What people are saying about …

D0071502

truereligion

"*True Religion* will wake up the passion sleeping in your soul. If your heart and soul have been cold to the trouble in this world, then you must read this book. Palmer Chinchen challenges armchair quarterbacks everywhere to get off the couch and give their lives away to change what is broken in this world."

Kurt Warner, NFL quarterback
and two-time league MVP

"What medicine would you prescribe for what ails the church? I'd suggest a strong dose of what Palmer Chinchen serves up in this book. Reading *True Religion* will transform lives—and entire congregations. This book should be required reading for twenty-first-century Christians."

Duane Litfin, president of Wheaton College

"We all owe a debt of gratitude to Palmer for taking us beyond the stagnation of self-absorbed spirituality to the joy of pouring our lives out to others in radical ways. If you're wondering what's missing in life, *True Religion* just may be your answer!"

Joseph Stowell, president of
Cornerstone University

"Warning: This book will disturb you. It also may change your life and your lifestyle for the better. Palmer Chinchen comes from a family who did give up their lives and change their lifestyles for the sake of others because of the gospel. This focus on others saturates Palmer's book. May it come to saturate your life and mine as well."

Dr. Robert (Ric) C. Cannada Jr., chancellor and CEO of Reformed Theological Seminary

"*True Religion* reminds me that to be Christlike means to be bothered by injustice. Palmer's true stories soften my heart toward the lost and the hurting and make me excited to give generously, just as Christ gives generously to me."

JJ Heller, singer and songwriter

taking pieces
of heaven

truereligion

to places of
hell on earth

Palmer Chinchen, PhD

David C Cook
transforming lives together

TRUE RELIGION
Published by David C. Cook
4050 Lee Vance View
Colorado Springs, CO 80918 U.S.A.

David C. Cook Distribution Canada
55 Woodslee Avenue, Paris, Ontario, Canada N3L 3E5

David C. Cook U.K., Kingsway Communications
Eastbourne, East Sussex BN23 6NT, England

David C. Cook and the graphic circle C logo
are registered trademarks of Cook Communications Ministries.

Some names mentioned throughout this book have
been changed for privacy purposes.

The Web site addresses recommended throughout this book are offered as a
resource to you. These Web sites are not intended in any way to be or imply an
endorsement on the part of David C. Cook, nor do we vouch for their content.

All Scripture quotations, unless otherwise noted, are taken from the *Holy Bible, New
International Version*®. *NIV*®. Copyright © 1973, 1978, 1984 by International Bible
Society. Used by permission of Zondervan. All rights reserved. Scripture quotations
marked GNT are taken from the Good News Translation—Second Edition. ©
1992 by American Bible Society. Used by permission. Scripture quotations marked
MSG are taken from *THE MESSAGE*. Copyright © by Eugene H. Peterson 1993,
1994, 1995, 1996, 2000, 2001, 2002. Used by permission of NavPress Publishing
Group. Scripture quotations marked NASB are taken from the *New American
Standard Bible,* © Copyright 1960, 1995 by The Lockman Foundation. Used
by permission. Scripture quotations marked NLT are taken from the New Living
Translation of the Holy Bible. New Living Translation copyright © 1996, 2004
by Tyndale Charitable Trust. Used by permission of Tyndale House Publishers.
The author has added italics to Scripture quotations for emphasis.

LCCN 2010924059
ISBN 978-0-7814-0343-6
eISBN 978-1-4347-0223-4

© 2010 Palmer Chinchen
Published in association with the literary agency of Creative Trust,
Inc., 5141 Virginia Way, Suite 320, Brentwood, TN 37027.

The Team: John Blase, Sarah Schultz, Caitlyn York, Karen Athen
Cover design: Amy Kiechlin
Cover images: iStockPhoto, royalty-free
Interior illustrations: Scott Erickson

Printed in the United States of America
First Edition 2010

1 2 3 4 5 6 7 8 9 10

032910

DEDICATION

This book is dedicated to my family ... all of them.

To my sweet and incredibly beautiful wife,
Veronica.
Without her encouragement and deep faith
I could do little of significance in life.

To my four sons,
Byron, Spencer, Christian, and William,
who make life magical.

To my parents,
Jack and Nell,
whose lives have inspired mine.

To my brothers and sisters who have been so supportive—
Del and Becky, Lisa and Steve, Paul and Laura, Marion
and Steve—and remind me that no one does it alone.

CONTENTS

ACKNOWLEDGMENTS

I first want to say a heartfelt thank-you to Kathryn Helmers, my agent, who saw something worthy in my writing before anyone else. I am so privileged to work with a true literary who is without question the finest agent working today.

I am deeply grateful to Don Pape, who invited me to be a part of everything exciting that is happening at David C. Cook. I also want to thank my editor, John Blase, as well as Terry Behimer and everyone else at Cook; you inspire me.

It's a privilege to be a part of everything exciting Dan Raines and his team are doing at Creative Trust. And a million thanks to Jim Chaffee for believing in this book and my story.

I also feel honored to pastor The Grove. Every Sunday is an adventure. No one could ask to pursue God with a more passionate people. Thank you for allowing me to express through the art of writing as I lead.

Finally, I want to thank all my coworkers at The Grove who have been so encouraging. God, in His supernatural way, has given us an incredibly gifted team: Jennifer Bellinger, Gary Bradley, Paul Gunther, Colby Martin, Rhoda Nyrienda, Joel Pritchard, Becky Schnee, Matt Shively, Shelia Smith, Matt Stowell, Ashley Page, Jared Zimmerman, and Mark Zurowski.

CONFESSION

Some moments last a lifetime.

I had a moment like that my senior year in high school in Liberia.

Our dorm parent, Mike, was driving a van of half a dozen high schoolers to our Wednesday night Bible study, when suddenly the small yellow taxi in front of us swerved off the road.

Taxis in Monrovia, Liberia's capital, are a piece of work. Most are used imports from Japan. They're small sedans made by Mitsubishi, Datsun (back in the day), or Toyota. Stripped down to the bare essentials for cheap sales in the developing world, these sedans would never be allowed on American roads. They land in Africa with over one hundred thousand miles on them. The brakes are a mess. The tires are misaligned. The wipers just smear the grime on the glass when it rains ... but the horns always blow. And each has been labeled across the trunk with the driver's favorite moniker: *Beezah in Worry; Grownah Peekin; God Can't Sleep; Beat It—Driver Beat It; Experience Never Suffer.*

With Bob Marley blaring, fuzzy dice hanging on the rearview mirror, tint so dark you can hardly see the sun, and a cloud of smoke filling the car from his filterless, hand-rolled cigarette—the driver can barely see what's happening around him. Especially since he has seven people crammed into his taxi to maximize profit. Two squeeze into the bucket seat up front, one has half a backside on the gear stick, and four more wedge into the rear seat. No seat belts, no air bags.

We watched in stunned horror as the crammed taxi careened off the road and launched off a large mound of dirt. The small sedan was ramped into the air, directly into a steel telephone pole. The impact with the pole flung the car sideways, and as it landed, it rolled violently before stopping on its roof.

The scene was horrific. I could only hope that someone survived. I jumped toward the door, grabbed the handle, and got ready to open it, but we kept going.

"Mike," I shouted, "stop the van!" I thought he must have somehow missed seeing the accident; he didn't turn his head or answer. "Mike, Mike!"

Now practically everyone was yelling for Mike to stop, but he didn't so much as slow down. We were angry and questioning his sanity.

"Mike, what are you thinking? Stop the van! Didn't you see the accident?"

I was only seventeen. I'm not sure what I could have done to help, but I did know that Mike had been a paramedic before moving to Africa.

Mike never stopped. He wouldn't answer. Finally, after several minutes, when we were well past the accident and the van had quieted, Mike stated matter-of-factly, "I didn't stop because I'm sure I would have had to give someone mouth-to-mouth resuscitation—and tonight I don't feel like giving anyone mouth-to-mouth resuscitation."

That was it.

At seventeen years old, I made a promise to myself: I would live differently.

———◆———

My name is Palmer Chinchen, and I'm an expatriate.

I've spent about half my life in Africa. Growing up, my home was the Liberian jungle. As an adult, I've taught college, preached, served, and lived in Liberia and then again across the continent in Malawi; I've also traveled to the ends of the continent and what feels like everywhere in between—from Cape Town to Cairo, from Dakar to Dar es Salaam.

The other half of my life, I've been in America, where I spend much of my time imploring others to give their lives away to love a hurting world. Over the years, I've invited others to travel with me to places far and away, like Guinea and Guatemala, Costa Rica and Cuba, Zimbabwe and Zambia.

I've written this book because I'm still bothered. The more I go and the I more see, the more I realize this world is broken and filled with people who hurt—filled with places of hell on earth. But it doesn't have to be this way. And that's what really gets me.

I—we—have the ability and resources to do so much. So much more than we do. Not only can we make a difference as individuals, but think about the combined power of a church or community or town or city. In the places on earth where children have no shoes, families have no homes, people have no hope— one person or one church can do much to fill the most miserable place with beauty.

I've written this book because my heart has been beating too fast lately. It happens when I lie in bed at night and the pressure of a busy pastorate becomes too much. Maybe you've been there with me. When life—the deadlines, the frantic pace, the unanswered emails, the kids' soccer schedule, the blaring TV, the nonstop texts, iChats, Facebook, Twitter—has squeezed in around you so tight you feel like your ribs are about to break and you can't even breathe.

And if it's not the zoo of life that gets you, then it's the treadmill that turns your soul comfortably numb. You know what I mean—if you've ever felt like you're suffocating in your cubicle, or you've sat in traffic, sucking fumes from cars all around and feeling as though there's not air enough to fill your lungs. Or if you've found the routine of life so catatonic that you wonder if you're still alive.

Breathe.

Breathe deep.

I've found that when I board a jumbo jet I can breathe.

Have you noticed that, as the jet climbs, something dramatic happens? Your perspective changes. Life looks different, life feels different; life is different. Inexplicably, troubles and worries shrink. What seemed dire just moments ago drifts into trivia. The squabble with a coworker, the leaking oil pan, the loud neighbor, the missed promotion, the loss on the stock market, the overcharge on your cell phone bill … all seem so very small now.

Because when you get on a plane and look down on this world, you see the grand picture; you get a glimpse of God's vantage from heaven.

At thirty-five thousand feet, you start to dream of a way life could be. You begin to see everything you never had time to do. You can picture yourself doing what everyone said was impossible.

I hope this book fills your lungs with life and lets you breathe again. There is so much more that God waits to do in and through you.

I'm a pastor, a writer, and an educator; however, I hope my life is mostly about the business of living out *true religion*—taking pieces of heaven to the places of hell on earth.

Because one day, I hope to hear two simple words: *Well done!*

How about you?

INTRO

ONE THOUSAND PERCENT; GO!

The Boeing 737 leveled off, floating effortlessly, almost silently, through the morning sky. As we leaned back to relax on our flight home from Havana, one of our college musicians turned to me and said, "Palmer, I have been a Christian my entire life. I grew up going to church. I went to a Christian high school and to Wheaton College, but this is the first time in my life that the God of the universe stepped down out of heaven and into the life of Paul Duncan."

"One thousand percent; *do not go!*"

The words hit my heart with a thud. I was certain God was leading me to Cuba, but now I heard this? Two weeks earlier, I had been weighing where to lead our College Ministry on its next missions trip. We had been to Costa Rica, Mexico, and hurricane-ravaged South Florida, but I felt God leading me to take the group somewhere American college students had never been. As I prayed, I looked up at the map of the world I kept above my desk, a daily reminder that the church is not limited to our building at the corner of Main Street and Union. My eye caught on the Communist island nation of Cuba. *Wow,* I thought, *I know of no one who has been there. Is there a way to take a team of college students to Cuba next summer?* The more I thought and prayed about it, the more I felt the rush of God telling me, *Go!*

To explore the possibility, I began calling pastor friends and asking if they knew anyone who had been to Cuba. I was soon given the name of the president of a Christian organization located just a few miles away. I was told this gentleman had been to Cuba recently and should be able to give me a good read on the feasibility of taking college students to the Communist country.

I immediately called him and excitedly blurted out my aspirations of leading a team of college students to Cuba. He listened quietly until I was done, then with calm certainty said, "My advice to you, Palmer, is *one thousand percent; do not go!* Taking college students to Cuba would be the worst mistake you ever make in ministry."

I was floored. He had to certainly believe that if we went to Cuba we would be persecuted, thrown in prison, maybe even killed. But I was not sure why he was so adamant. So I pressed, "Why do you say, 'Do not go?'"

"Three reasons," he quickly replied. "One, the hotel room they put us in had no air conditioning—and Palmer, you talk about hot and humid! Two, the food was awful. We had beans for breakfast, beans for lunch, and beans for dinner. Worst food I've ever had. And three … I stepped on a rusty nail!"

I waited … then said, "Is that it?" That was it! I'm not kidding you. I hung up and exhaled, "Thank You, God, we're going to Cuba!" His xenophobia had made up my mind. If all we had to worry about were beans, air conditioning, and rusty nails … then by all means, we were going to Cuba. Six months later I had the exhilarating experience of leading twenty-one college students on a life-changing experience behind the sugarcane curtain.

———◆———

Paul Duncan would never be the same. He has since committed his life to full-time music ministry. I saw the same happen in the lives of many on the Cuba teams that followed. Dan and Corrie moved to Africa. Swanie went to Arizona to become a youth pastor. Lincoln returned to Trinidad and Tobago to preach. Josh gave his life to the pastorate. And Brian quit his job and moved to Ventura to lead a ministry to students.

GIVE YOUR LIFE AWAY

We live in a self-indulgent culture. Much of life is arranged for the good of ourselves. So we accumulate, we chase leisure and pleasure, we self-promote, and we do all we can to point the world at *me*. But God lays out a different way of living that is better for His world and better for you. Give your life away to change this world for good.

Christ made a profound request of you and me and everyone else who determines to walk in His footsteps: "Take up [your] cross and follow Me."[1]

The appeal is an interesting one, because on His cross He gave His life away to change this world—to change your life and my life—forever. He knows this planet we live on contains ruined places and rubbish-filled lives. But it doesn't have to be that way. He asks that you continue to carry His cross and do good, share hope, show love, and bring healing.

Quoting the ancient prophet Isaiah, the Christ stated His movement manifesto like this: "Preach good news to the poor.... Proclaim freedom for the prisoners and recovery of sight for the blind, [and] release the oppressed."[2]

Jesus never made this life about what He could gain for Himself. He was never interested in power or control or recognition or fame or possessions. He was oddly focused on rescuing other people from oppressive regimes, social stigmas, broken marriages, crippled bodies, physical blindness, and spiritual death.

He succeeded.

But upon His departure, He asked that you and I pick up the cross He once bore and carry it for Him.

AND GOD WILL CHANGE YOU

Here's the kicker: Give your life away to change this world, and *God will change you*. Something transformational happens in our lives when we go and give them away.

Every time I lead people on global ministry experiences, I see lives radically changed practically before my eyes. I watch challenging situations and disturbing moments transform people forever. The Havana team's experience was not unique. A clear pattern exists, giving a strong foundation to the idea that global experiences have a unique, powerful, life-altering effect on the spiritual condition of participants.

The Wheaton College School of Business sent a questionnaire out to graduates from the past five years. It included the question, "What aspect of your college experience had the greatest spiritual influence on your life?" An overwhelming majority of graduates indicated a global cross-cultural experience. Not the chapel services, not the Bible classes, not the dorm small groups, not even the college pastor down the street (ouch, that hurt)—but the experience of giving their lives away to a hurting world.

Over the course of my fifteen years in college ministry, I have led hundreds of students on cross-cultural service experiences: orphanage teams to Mexico, soccer teams to Costa Rica, evangelistic teams to Guatemala, basketball teams to Cuba, construction teams to Liberia, music teams to Malawi, relief teams to Mississippi (yes, taking college students from Los Angeles to rural Mississippi was definitely cross-cultural), and the list goes on. And in each experience, the lives of students were radically transformed.

———

Allison's life was spiraling. Not only was she drinking at parties, now she was hiding alcohol in her bedroom and drinking in solitude. At eighteen she was slipping into alcoholism. On top of this, she had started to experiment with drugs.

Her parents could tell something was desperately wrong with their sweet, happy, always-smiling Allison. The laughter had died. They discovered bottles of alcohol in her room and threw them out, but she just bought more. Finally Allison agreed to check into rehab. Little changed.

One Sunday morning, during the summer she graduated from high school, I stopped her and said, "Allison, you need to come to Africa." Her eyes lit up. She immediately answered with a perky, "I will."

Some questioned the wisdom of taking a girl who had her own problems all the way to Africa to help a troubled world. But I insisted this was the right decision.

Allison was inspirational. She poured her heart into the lives of orphans that summer. Her enthusiasm was absolutely contagious.

When she returned, all she could talk about was going back. I sensed that, for the first time in years, she realized her life contained something valuable. She had something worth giving that orphans in Africa treasured—love.

Her struggles in life were not over, but God had a new grip on her heart. After her first year of college she left the country again, this time for six months in Australia and Africa. The desire to fill her body with substances was replaced by a desire for more of God. She filled her life with Him, and He filled her heart with new passion and new desires.

Allison returned a different person. She leaves for Africa again next month. Allison's become the expatriate.

TRANSFORMING MOMENTS

Princeton professor James Loder writes about the nature of Christian transformation.[3] He uses his own near-death experience in an automobile accident as an example of the power of a transforming event. God uses conflicts of the soul, even accidents, to shape spirituality. His Spirit works through transforming moments to cause your spirituality to come alive, to be new.

Far too many Christians spend countless years at the same level of spiritual maturity, never growing deeper, never moving forward, never accomplishing more for Christ, never experiencing the life of great faith. This is why transforming moments are so necessary.

The busyness of life often creates a frantic pace that leads nowhere. We become lost in the rat race of work, or the confusion of taxiing children from soccer practice to cheer, to violin, to karate ... and are drained of any passion or time for deeper spirituality.

A transforming experience wakes up your soul. Your eyes open wide as you soak in all that God can do through you. You now see the limitless potential you possess. Your senses are keener than ever before; you hear His still, small voice, and you know He listens to your every whisper. You develop a passion for life and God like you have never known. Your vision for life has increased and intensified.

In the New Testament accounts, we see Saul the Christ-rebel hit by a transforming moment. He's headed down the road of animosity and anger when God rocks his world. He knocks Saul flat on his face ... and lights up his dark soul.

Blinded by God, Saul would become Paul and never see the same again.

We had a moment like this in Cuba.

————◆————

"You don't have visas? Then you'll have to sleep on the airport floor and fly back tomorrow." The Cuban customs official at the José Martí Airport in Havana meant business. I thought about arguing, but images of Communist gulags and waterboarding kept me silent.

The official was right; we had no visas because my contact in Havana, a Pastor David, had not shown up when we landed! We had a week of performances scheduled in Santiago de Cuba, but now we couldn't even enter the country.

But this was my third experience in Cuba and I knew one thing for sure: Cubans love music! So I found our percussion player, Lincoln from Trinidad and Tobago, and said, "Bro, pull the band together; you play, and we'll pray."

Maybe it was both the music and the prayer that softened the spirit of the customs chief. Half an hour later he called me into his office and said, "I can allow you to enter the country on visitors' visas, but your band cannot play any concerts until our headquarters in Havana grants your religious visas."

We spent the night in Havana and flew on to Santiago the next day. We were glad to be in Cuba but greatly disappointed that we could not share our music and words of hope. We made contact with Pastor David on the phone and found out his car had broken down on the way to the airport. He told us the customs department had denied our request for religious visas and we would not be able to perform publicly.

The next day, we gathered at a small Christian seminary and sat down with several dozen students to pray, asking God to intervene and grant our visas. Less than an hour into our time of prayer, our host, Pastor Joel, was summoned into the next room for a phone call. A few minutes later, he returned and interrupted our prayer: "That was the customs department in Havana. The official on the phone has told me that the Strongman says you may perform your concerts."

CHANGES

You want to change the world? Travel the world, and it will change you.

My entire point is this: If you will give your life away to changing this world, God will change you. This book is about the exhilarating transformation God works in you spiritually when you live that way.

The global experience will disturb your soul and change your spiritual state. You will have new eyes, you will have a softened heart, you will have an "upsized" idea of God, you will love people in new ways, you will be bothered by things you never noticed before, you will discover the ability to do things you never believed you could do, and your life will never be the same.

James Fowler is considered the preeminent thinker on faith-development theory. Fowler uses the idea of stages to describe the development process of spiritual maturity.[4] In much the same way that Jean Piaget constructed the idea that people develop physically and cognitively in stages and Lawrence Kohlberg explained how we develop morally in stages, Fowler applies developmental theory to the faith maturation process. In other words, when we develop spiritually, this development happens in defined, sequential, and identifiable stages.[5]

Developmental theorists talk about five aspects of the human personality. In the field of faith development, Christian thinkers like Perry Downs, James Fowler, and Linda Canal explain that our faith grows, matures, develops, and deepens in these same life-areas: (1) Moral: We grow in our moral conscience. For example, we become increasingly aware of injustice, oppression, and racism. (2) Cognitive: We develop a deeper understanding of God and His plan for humanity. (3) Physical: Our faith has a "doing" component. Faith becomes not just something we believe; it's something we do. (4) Emotional: Our passions and desires change as we mature in our relationship with God. (5) Relational: People have a dramatic influence on our spiritual formation.

Together we will explore how living globally and giving our lives away alters the shape of each of these areas of spiritual formation.

———

For centuries the Jewish people have repeated the same phrase from the Hebrew Bible; they call it the *Shema*. These words are woven into the fabric of Jewish life. Children know the words by heart; adults treasure them like precious stones.

Moses first wrote the words in the Torah, and Jesus later repeated them like this:

*Hear, O Israel, The L*ORD *our God, the*
*L*ORD *is one.*
*Love the L*ORD *your God with all your* heart
and with all your soul
and with all your mind
and with all your strength.
The second is this: 'Love your neighbor *as yourself.*[6]

Of all the Hebrew words, the word *shema* is the most weighted to the Jew. No other word is so deep with meaning and tradition. Some call it "the greatest text of monotheism."[7] Following God wholeheartedly starts here. The Israelites believed that God's most precious instructions for life were found in the text of the Shema.

The word *shema* means "to hear," and the Shema begins with the word *hear.* In other words—sit up and take notice; what God is about to say here is incredibly important.

So twice a day, the devout Jews say the Shema: at daybreak and sunset. Over the centuries, some have been so eager to recite these first words of the day that rabbis have had to qualify what constitutes the beginning of a new day; they've finally agreed on the stipulation that, until there is enough daylight to distinguish the color blue from white on the prayer shawl, one cannot recite the Shema.[8]

But hearing or saying the Shema is not enough. The Shema is meant to be lived. If you love God, if you know God, you will *do* the Shema.

Here's what's so beautiful about the Shema: It explains that God wants your love. He's not just interested in your obedience; He wants your heart. That's the sweet essence of the Shema.

But this is possibly why the Shema has become one of the most treasured nuggets of God's Word—it holds the answer to the question all people of all time have asked:

What is the most important thing I must do with my life?

With just five powerful words, the Shema says it like this: Love the Lord your God with all your *mind, heart, soul, strength* … and love your *neighbor.*

These words were not meant to be regulations or rules; the words of the Shema are a way *to* life.

A way to really live.

The way to love God so that our religion is *true.*

These five components of the Shema will inform and give structure to our exploration of spiritual transformation. You will discover the surprising ways that God takes the life-given-away and turns it into something even more beautiful.

Read on. You will be changed.

Ideas for Becoming the Expatriate

Eat out at ethnic restaurants (Panda Express, Del Taco, and Olive Garden don't count). Thai food is off the hook. And if you can find a Cuban or Brazilian restaurant, you are in for an amazing experience.

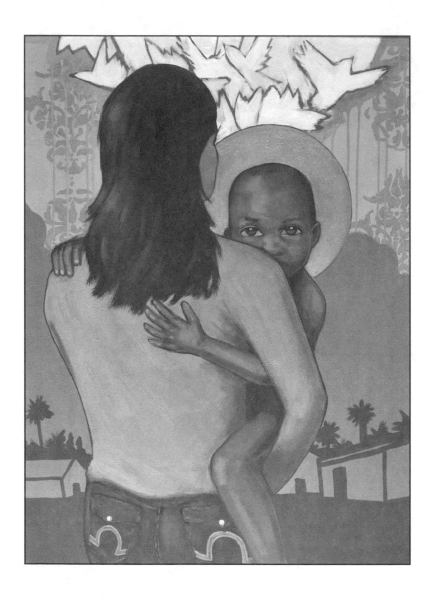

PART I

EXPATRIATE

Love the Lord your God with all your soul.

AIDS first ravaged the body of Mulungu's father and stole his life. Mulungu's mother was left behind, now penniless with two children to feed and clothe—and with the curse of a disease that has no cure. Her body shriveled. She could hardly pull herself out of bed. At eight years old, Mulungu became the man of the house. He dressed and fed his little sister, cooked the food, cared for his dying mother … but as hard as he tried, he couldn't stop her life from slipping away.

Mulungu and his sister became two more of the nearly one million orphans in the country of Malawi.

Out of community and family obligation, his uncle came for them and took them to live in his village. But his uncle's home, like so many others, was overrun with his own children along with orphans of other dead relatives. Besides, he was a peasant farmer, barely growing enough maize to keep his own family alive.

Mulungu and his sister were fed last, and they were fed less. Hunger was real, every day, all day. Mulungu began stealing food from his uncle's home. Enraged, the uncle responded by taking him out and chaining the eight-year-old boy to a tree. He lived chained there for days and weeks. His sister kept him alive by sneaking her own food to him.

Local tobacco farmers finally noticed Mulungu chained in the field and notified a local orphan ministry, Children of the Nations. My close friend Chris Clark, who founded COTN, cannot tell the story without tears filling his eyes. When they arrived, Mulungu looked like a chained dog; he was starving to death.

They unchained him and took him to their home.

CHAPTER 1

TRUE RELIGION

I believe God wants us all to live bothered by things around us that are not right. The world is a broken place, and He has put you and me here to make it whole. Possibly the most important indicator of true religion is the desire to love and care for people who hurt.

TRUES

Some friends told me about a brand of jeans that is popular with the Hollywood crowd and the fabulously rich; it's called True Religion. I stopped and looked at some in a store the other day—the price tag read $348. That might become your religion if you spent so much on jeans, but that certainly is not *true* religion.

Jesus' brother James said it like this: "Religion that God our Father accepts as pure and faultless [true religion] is this: to look after orphans and widows in their distress."[1]

Can I just say if I were to ever spend $348 on a pair of jeans, then I would have lost all bearing on life? Seriously, if children in Malawi are being chained to trees because there's not enough food to go around, or if Africa is filled with children living bare naked because they have no clothes … then how on earth could I make any sense of spending $348 on jeans?

True religion is more about others and less about me. Living out true religion means I've stopped being so concerned about what I want and what I get, and I spend my days caring about what others don't have and what others need. The Christian life is meant to be that way.

Jesus explained true religion like this: "Whenever you feed the hungry, clothe the poor, give water to the thirsty, visit the imprisoned, or loved the unloved—you love Me!"[2]

My favorite introspective writer, Brennan Manning, observes, "Jesus spent a disproportionate amount of time with people described in the gospels as: the poor, the blind, the lame, the lepers, the hungry, sinners, prostitutes, tax collectors, the persecuted, the downtrodden, the captives, those possessed by unclean spirits, all who labor and are heavy burdened, the rabble who know nothing of the law, the crowds, the little ones, the least, the last, and the lost sheep of the house of Israel…. In short, Jesus hung out with ragamuffins."[3]

So, in the name of Jesus, give your life away to love people who hurt! God wants everyday people like you and me to be His hands and feet. So go! Love the marginalized, free the oppressed, show mercy to the hurting, give to the poor, feed the hungry, love the orphans and the widows, and take good news to the lost.

MARGINS

Jesus always seemed to notice when people were pushed into the margins. They are still there today. But too often they are the invisible ones. We pass them and don't know their names. We don't stop to ask about their pain. They are the forgotten ones.

Jesus lived bothered by abuse, injustice, and oppression.

On one occasion, a crowd of men came to Him, planning to stone a woman accused of adultery. Jesus' eyes pierced the men surrounding the shamed woman. She stood guilty of adultery and infidelity. But Christ stood close to her. His fists were clenched, His words were curt: "Let the one who has never sinned throw the first stone."[4]

The silence was deafening. He slowly bent down and wrote with His finger. Were they words of compassion He wrote? Was it a line from the Torah? Theologians have debated the words in the sand for centuries. Personally, I believe he wrote this: "The first one of you who dares to throw a rock at this beautiful woman ... I will personally beat you down!" Okay, I'm probably wrong, but I like the thought, and I might be close. I feel this way because His attitude toward injustice was always—*NO WAY! Not on My watch; not as long as I am here.*

This must be our attitude as well. We must develop a moral conscience. Injustice should gnaw at our souls. Begin to be bothered by situations that are not right. Start speaking up when things are not right. This is what the Lord requires of His followers.

We all need to live a bit more bothered when something is wrong with this world.

MORAL DILEMMAS

Christians talk a lot about conversion and change. An important aspect of the change that must take place in the believer's life is moral transformation. All people are created with a moral dimension to their human personality. In much the same way we grow and change physically, we also develop morally.

Donal Dorr, who writes extensively on the need for a balanced faith that addresses issues of justice, says we need a *moral conversion*.[5] Because sometimes Christians have a conversion of the intellect, but their souls remain callused to what is not right in this world.

Harvard University professor Lawrence Kohlberg developed the idea of Stages of Moral Development. He explains that people develop morally in stages.[6] For example, children do not understand or comprehend justice the way adults should; that's why two-year-olds always say, *"Mine!"* We're supposed to outgrow that.

The problem is that as Christians we often only teach moral knowledge. But unfortunately, moral knowledge does not always lead to moral action. The moral conscience can be scarred, calloused, or ignored. For example, the religious leaders of Jesus' day knew the Hebrew Bible inside and out, yet Jesus said if they were to see a bleeding man on the side of the road, they would walk on by. Their spirituality was not *true religion*.

The ancient Jewish prophet Micah wrote about true religion, religion that makes the heart of God smile: "He has shown all you people what is good. And what does the LORD require of you? To act justly and to love mercy and to walk humbly with your God."[7]

Jesus described His own purpose and mission as this: "He has anointed me to preach good news to the poor. He has sent me to proclaim freedom for the prisoners and recovery of sight for the blind, to release the oppressed."[8]

I would argue then that moral transformation often comes when we are willing to step outside our places of comfort and safety and not just *think* morally but *do* morally. When you give your life away to this world, when you live out your religion as God intended, you open your life to being stunned by God and your moral character to being transformed.

The world is filled with places and actions that are unjust and oppressive. A primary Christian duty is to put an end to these practices. Live convinced that you can change what is wrong in this world and make it just a little bit more beautiful.

UNSILENCED

My friend Scott Erickson, who paints images that are branded on his heart from his travels to Cameroon, says he paints so that his art becomes a voice for all in Africa who have been silenced.

Part of our Christian duty is to become a *prophetic voice.* By this I mean you and I speaking out, as the ancient Jewish prophets did, against practices that are not right.

The work of Brazilian educator Paulo Freire has revolutionized the way Christian educators talk about our moral duty. Frustrated with Brazil's oppressive educational system, Freire began promoting the idea of *conscientization*.[9]

Conscientization is the process by which people become aware of practices around them that are dehumanizing. People must first realize their oppression before they can confront it and overcome it. Liberation comes through conscientization. The more people understand their oppression, the more they become human. And once the marginalized can name and verbalize the oppression, they become empowered to take part in confronting, speaking out against, and reshaping that reality.

But you don't have to go to the Democratic Republic of Congo or Sudan to see oppressive practices that need your voice.

The first time I passed a sheriff's chain gang in Arizona, I couldn't believe what I was seeing. Women in prison-striped uniforms hoeing weeds ... chained at the ankles, with shotgun-toting deputies standing watch. I was shocked. It looked like a scene from 1950s rural America.

My soul ached to the gut. Yes, these women may have committed crimes that deserved incarceration—but not this dehumanizing humiliation. I hurt for them. I wanted to cry for them. My thought was, "Palmer, you must do something ..." So I hung a U and got out. I approached the deputy and asked if he would give a message to the sheriff. He listened patiently as I said, "Please tell your sheriff that in Chandler, we do not want women humiliated. In Chandler, we believe that every person should be treated with dignity and respect. In Chandler, we want this practice stopped." He was kind enough to say he would pass my message along.

All human beings have great worth. Regardless of race, gender, ability, wealth, religion, or nationality, all people deserve dignity and respect. This is not only a Christian argument or position. This is a moral position. To publicly humiliate another person is immoral and unjust. It's wrong at every level.

Who among us would stand idly by while a person maliciously scarred da Vinci's *Mona Lisa* with graffiti? We would scream *NO! Stop!* We would take action because this painting is deemed beautiful and priceless. How much more beautiful and priceless is the life of a woman—even one in chains!

The Christian today must be aware of the pain that society, consciously or unconsciously, imposes on people. The suffering is real, it hurts, and it's time to stop it.

RESPOND

Solomon, in his great wisdom, explained that empathizing with those who hurt is not enough: "Speak up for those who cannot speak for themselves, for the rights of all who are destitute. Speak up and judge fairly; defend the rights of the poor and needy."[10]

About twenty of us Chinchens were standing under the shade of a giant tree at Disney World trying to decide where to head next, when, just a few feet away, I noticed a young couple arguing loudly. I turned just in time to watch him raise his hand high and slap her hard across the face.

I couldn't believe what I just witnessed. Without thinking, I reacted by grabbing him from behind.… Okay, I realize this was not a pastoral response, but I've got some Scotch-Irish in my blood.

"What are you thinking?! You can't hit her!" I blurted out.

"She was asking for it," he mumbled, still in my grip.

"Well, not here," I stated with conviction. "Never, ever again will you hit her. Is that clear?"

I'm not sure if it was the headlock or my convincing words, but he agreed.

Anywhere in the world, slapping a woman is despicable ... especially at the happiest place on earth!

———

As I said earlier, Christian morality is not simply about having good judgment on issues of right and wrong; it's more about moral action—doing what is right.

In the late 1960s, John Darley and Bibb Latané were the first researchers to do extensive studies on the psychological phenomenon of noninvolvement, or why people fail to help when someone is in distress.

Darley and Latané found several reasons why bystanders will simply watch a person drown, for example, and do nothing. One is stage fright: "I may appear foolish if they really do not need help." Another reason is risk: "They may pull me under, and I may drown with them." Still another reason is deferred involvement: "If others are not helping, I guess I don't need to help."[11]

Here's what's most bizarre. The more people present, the less likely it becomes that someone will help! Researchers have put children on the streets of both cities and small towns and had them say to passing strangers, "I'm lost. Can you help me?" People in cities like New York kept walking. I'm not kidding. People in small towns were far more likely to help. The researchers found that it's better to be desperate in a small town—with fewer people—than in a city, especially New York, with many passersby.

We can live a lifetime that way. We can see pictures of enslaved women chained to trees in Sudan and say, "That's sad. I'm sure the UN will put a stop to that." Or we can watch CNN and see men eating dirt out of cans in Malawi to ease their hunger pangs and think, *That's not good. I'm sure World Vision will ship in some rice.* We do this never realizing the responsibility may be ours!

———

I was glad to be getting out of Kenya. The country had been going through months of civil unrest. For the first time in decades, Kenya had become a place of violence. Neighbors who had lived for years peacefully next door to one another were now turning on each other because of tribal differences. The mood of the country surprised even Kenyans.

I woke up early to catch my flight to Monrovia and left my hotel by six thirty. But as my taxi driver drove past Nairobi's central park, it was already filling with riot police and water-cannon trucks. In spite of the government's objections, a new political party was planning demonstrations for this day, and no one expected them to be peaceful. I was really glad to be getting out of Kenya.

We made our way onto the four-lane road that leads to the Nairobi airport and were doing about sixty when the minivan in front of us abruptly changed lanes, striking the rear quarter panel of a minibus to its left. The minibus was packed full of passengers, at least a dozen. The minibus swerved left, then right, then violently flipped onto its side. It skidded before rolling onto its roof, which immediately collapsed.

I have to be honest—when I saw the minibus full of people crash onto its roof, my first thought was, *Let's get out of Kenya. Riots are coming. If you stop you may miss your flight. The road is busy with cars; of course others will stop to help. Palmer, you don't have to get involved.*

But of all thoughts, in that nanomoment, my mind raced back twenty-plus years to the memory of Mike driving past the upside-down taxi. And I remembered my promise: *I will live differently.*

"Driver, stop the car!" I shouted with urgency. We both jumped out running. He was a Christian too; we had been listening to praise songs in Swahili.

The collapsed roof had smashed every window in the van. The openings were now barely wide enough to pull people out. Others joined us as we took people by their arms or legs and eased them through the shattered glass. Within just a couple of minutes everyone was out. Some had minor cuts or bruises to their heads, but miraculously no one appeared critically injured.

Just as I was feeling relieved, my driver shouted, "They're beating the other driver!" I turned to see a mob attacking the driver who had caused the accident. Some were kicking him in the head, others punching, some throwing huge stones.

In Africa they call it mob justice. If you hit a pedestrian with your car, the mob will beat you to death. If you steal a shirt off a neighbor's clothesline, the mob will chase you and beat you to death.

It's become a senseless form of law enforcement that, unfortunately, unemployed young men seem to take pleasure in.

With my driver shouting at the mob in Swahili, I ran into the midst and dropped to my knees and bent over the man to protect him from the blows. A thought flashed through my head—*I hope they don't turn on me.* Strangely, I did not feel afraid. I sensed that a man was dying, and I had to do whatever I could to save his life.

I looked up as one man buried his foot in the man's side, clasped my hands together in a sign of pleading, and yelled, "*Palebe, palebe!*" (In Chichewa, the national language of Malawi, where I had just been the day before, this means *please.* But now I was in Kenya, where they speak Swahili.) They seemed to know what I meant. Their faces were still filled with rage, but the kicking and punching stopped. The stones were dropped.

The angry men continued to argue with my driver in Swahili: "We want to kill him. He's a fool. He deserves to die!"

My driver was adamant in return. "No, you will not."

The man had been struck hard on the back of the head by a cement block. He was unconscious when I first bent over him. I held his head and began to say, "You have to get up, you can't stay here, they want to kill you." He regained consciousness, and I helped him sit up. I rubbed the debris from the back of his head and finally helped him to his feet. Then I waited till the mob dispersed.

Just the day before, I had been feeling sorry for myself because during this particular trip to Africa, I had missed my wedding anniversary, my son's eighteenth birthday, and a large, weeklong event at my church. But as we drove the rest of the way to the Nairobi Airport, the thought hit me that maybe this was the only place God wanted me. Because if God used me to save just one man's life, then it was worth everything I had left behind.

I'm not a hero, just a Christ-follower trying to do what I encourage others to do.

Give your life away.

Pour it into people.

Souls last forever.

Ideas for Becoming the Expatriate

Rent more movies with subtitles. France, India, and Japan, for example, are producing an increasing number of good films that rarely make it into American theaters.

CHAPTER 2

IT'S TIME TO LIVE DIFFERENTLY

The African sky grew dark as the tropical rain beat our house in torrents. My twenty-eight-year-old brother, Del, sat on the veranda with my twin brother, Paul, and me; Paul and I were in junior high at the time. We watched the display of lightning flash against the darkened horizon while dusk set in.

I've found that life's most vivid scenes never fade.

Suddenly, through the downpour, we saw a girl running toward us.

Sharing this story is difficult, and I don't mean to shock you with the details, but at thirteen years old, this was a defining moment for me. What happened next would shape the way I would live the rest of my life.

Her clothes were drenched, her head was down. I could see her long, blonde hair was tangled and matted from the pouring rain. As we got up to meet her I could hear her sobs as she ran closer. She clenched her torn shirt closed. Her white pants were ripped open and stained with blood.

When she came under the veranda, I recognized her. I had only been at the International School for a month, but I knew she was one of the ninth graders. Between her sobs, she moaned, "I've been raped … I've been raped."

My mother rushed outside, wrapped her arms around the girl, and held her for a moment. As she led the girl inside, Del stopped her and asked gently, "Where did this happen?"

She answered quietly, "I was walking home from the movie theater in the rain when a man ran up behind me, grabbed me by the hair, and dragged me to the soccer field, where he attacked me."

As my mother led her inside, Del looked at my brother and me and said, "Get in the car. Let's find him."

We ran through the rain to his VW bug. The soccer field was just several hundred yards away, across the street and down a short dirt road. Del drove like a man possessed. I felt his rage. I wanted nothing more than for us to find this vile man and make him pay. I wanted revenge. I wanted justice.

The muddy water splashed over the hood of the VW as we sped wildly down the dirt road. We scanned the roadside and bushes in hope of catching a glimpse of the rapist. At the soccer field, we jumped out and sprinted through the gates. There was no one.

We never found the man. All I felt was gut-sickening rage. I wanted justice. But what I wished most was that I had been close enough earlier to defend this beautiful girl.

A week later, she came back to school. I never saw her lift her downcast eyes. I never saw her smile again.

Sometimes people ask why I'm so bothered when women are treated badly. Maybe it started that dark day in Africa.

MARGINS

I believe we know deep inside that we are to respond to people who hurt. Why don't we live that way?

But when God really gets a hold of our lives, He makes us more keenly aware of what is right and what is wrong. He embeds this clear moral obligation in the creation of every person. And sometimes it takes a transforming experience to awaken us to this moral duty.

A key purpose of this book is to challenge you to develop a Christian response to poverty, injustice, and oppression.

The truth is, many people lack a well-thought-out, well-defined, well-processed theology of justice. Many of us just weren't raised in homes or churches that talked much about these things. As a result, we're not sure how to adequately respond to the problems of marginalization, abuse, and disease.

Bono has famously said, "There is a continent—Africa—being consumed by flames. When the history books are written, this generation will be known for the Internet, the war on terror, and what we did—or did not do—to put the fire out in Africa. We must engage as individuals and communities to confront these issues."[1]

I invite you to wrestle with these issues that plague the globe today: What will our response be to the problem of poverty that plagues our world? How will we respond to the problem of malaria in Africa, a preventable and eradicable disease that claims an African child's life every thirty seconds? What are we doing about the women sold as sex slaves in Somalia, Sudan, and Ethiopia? How about the AIDS crisis in Africa that claims six thousand Africans every day and has left millions of children orphaned? And what will our response be to oppressive governments and tyrannical regimes that strip people of their freedom and dignity and dehumanize women by treating them as inferior to men?

These moral problems should be important to you and me because they have always been important to God. They were important to Jesus Christ and the early church; why aren't they important to His people today?

PLACES IN THE PEW

If the twenty-first-century church is serious about being a church to the afflicted and oppressed, then we must recognize that a vast majority of the world's poor and hurting live across the oceans. This means we have to leave our places in the pew and spend time in the margins.

The Bible repeatedly demonstrates God's passion for justice. Oppression disturbs the heart of God. The cry for freedom originates with God Himself: "Let my people go!"[2] He is the God of liberation. He freed the Jewish people from Babylon; He freed Joseph from the pit; He freed Mordecai from the gallows; He freed Paul from a crumbling prison; He freed ten vagrants from leprosy; He freed Christ from the tomb; and He frees you and me for eternity.

Solomon makes this riveting appeal to God: "Make me the King of Justice!"[3] He asks that God empower him to defend the afflicted, save the children of the poor, crush the oppressor, save those who cry for help, rescue the dying, and end the violence. Because Solomon says, the marginalized are "precious ... in his sight."[4]

But understand this simple reality: When you commit to the margins, those in the middle will resist. The most affluent are not always the most compelled. People in the middle want the resources and programming and pastors of the church to benefit them. I cannot be less than painfully honest—some people would rather give money for new cribs in the nursery than give for beds to be built for orphans in Mozambique who sleep on hard dirt floors.

SLEEP AMERICA

In Arizona we have a mattress company named Sleep America. Its slogan sings: *Where America goes to sleep.*

We are a sleepy nation that loves all things soft. We buy shoes with the softest soles. We want cars with the softest ride. We install carpet that's soft on our feet. We squeeze toilet paper to make sure it will be soft to the touch. And we buy mattresses with the softest pillow top.

In much the same way, we expect a soft, comfortable faith, one that fits easily with soccer leagues, shopping malls, and vacations on the beach.

Jesus never promised faith would be soft and comfortable. He told us to take up our crosses and follow Him and said, "Foxes have holes and the birds of the air have nests, but the Son of Man has no place to lay his head."[5]

Luke tells of when Jesus asked His friends to pray for Him. The Christ's moment was dark; He felt desperate. Yet, as soon as He walked away to pray alone, they fell asleep! Jesus came back and couldn't believe it. When He needed them most, they napped.

I believe the same thing has happened with the church today. When the world needs us most, we have fallen asleep to global pain. As the imprisoned New Testament rebel Paul wrote, "Awake, sleeper, and arise from the dead, and Christ will shine on you."[6]

I have a friend who says every time she sees the woven mats laid out on the dirt floor of a Rwandan hut, she can't help but think of our Sleep Number Beds on the market. What number do you give a bamboo mat on a dirt floor?

Sean, who lived in Africa, says that he can't find the word *comfortable* in the Bible.

Maybe it's time to live a little less comfortable.

THE GLOBAL MESSAGE OF JESUS

After I returned from my second trip to Cuba with a team of college students, one of our church's leaders invited me to lunch. Soon after we sat down, I realized he had mail to deliver. He leaned over the table cloak-and-dagger-like, as though someone at the next table were there to record our conversation. In hushed tones, he murmured, "You've been taking students all over Africa and Cuba. We think there are too many risks. We believe something can go wrong, really wrong. I want to ask you to do this—keep your teams closer to home, stay just a bit closer to Chicago."

I liked his style, a bit KGB-esque. But liking his style and agreeing with him were two different things. I leaned across the table and answered, "I must go! There are thousands of Christians willing to stay close to home, but I know of none who are willing to carry the name of Christ to places like Cuba. No, I'm sorry, I cannot promise to stay close to home."

I had promised myself to live differently. Now it was time to lead differently.

That's what Jesus said He was here to do, "To preach good news to the poor…. Proclaim freedom for the prisoners and recovery of sight for the blind, [and] to release the oppressed."[7]

He came for everyone in the margins.

The cul-de-sac at the end of your street is not enough. The corner your church sits on is not enough. Begin to think globally, begin to live globally. Economically and technologically we have become a global society. The church must begin to think the same way. The Christian faith of the future will be shaped by what happens in Africa, Latin America, and Asia. The next revolution for God is out there … not in here.

EXPATRIATE

I've been using a word to describe the lives of people who leave their country to make home a far and away place. This one word describes an extraordinary life, a life of adventure, a life of uncertainty, a life of exhilaration, a life worth living. The word is *expatriate*.

Expatriates live differently. Expats (as expatriates are referred to in international circles) soak up the world in which they land. They don't try to take home with them. They absorb the smells. They soak up the uniqueness of the culture.

Expatriates are resilient. They have resolve and learn to adapt and improvise. They expect little. They find guilty pleasure in luxuries as simple as an air-conditioned restaurant, a hammock by the beach, an ice-cold Coca-Cola … in a glass bottle.

The Sandals all-inclusive frequenter is not the expatriate. The get-out-of-the-tour-bus-and-take pictures crowd is not the expatriate. The loud, obnoxious guy in the hotel swimming pool is not the expatriate. Becoming the expatriate involves a new way of living, a new way of thinking, a new way of believing, a new way of dreaming.

I've observed something true in practically all expats. Once they have tasted the haphazard, horn-honking, chickens-everywhere, annoying-venders, pungent-odor, soggy-air, crazed-taxi-drivers, drunk-policemen, disorienting, take-life-as-it-comes world away from home … they want more.

When expatriates return "home," their souls shrivel. They cringe at chain anything. The suburbs and minivans and strip malls and fast food suck their spirits dry. They can't wait to board the next plane to somewhere far and away.

And maybe life is better like that. This world is not for making home, so live on the go—go and live; really, really live.

It's time to live differently.

It's time to really live.

It's time to become the expatriate.

THE WORLD IS NOT ENOUGH

Sometimes people are glib to the world's plight.

When I return from Africa, I'm often greeted with the question, "So, did you have a *good* time in Africa?" The question is meant to be unassuming and usually wants little more than a superficial response. But I have been asked the question so many times it has caused me to pause: "Are you asking, 'Were the bouts with malaria, the violent fever and relentless nausea, *good?*' Are you asking, 'Was the *gangbah* (fermented cassava) with *boney* (dried fish) *good?*' Are you asking, 'Was being cramped in a minibus for hours, all the while wondering if you would contract TB, *good?*' Or are you asking 'Were the funeral services you performed for infants who died from the AIDS they contracted from their infected mothers *good?*'"

I'm not really sure how to respond anymore. Because there are many things that happen in Africa today that are not *good*, but aren't we supposed to go anyway?

———◆———

Not only are we often unaware of global problems, but some know little about the globe itself.

A true story circulated after the last Olympics held in the United States. A caller phoned the U.S. Olympic ticket line, hoping to purchase tickets. The ticket agent answered and asked, "Where are you calling from?"

"New Mexico," the caller answered.

"If you're from Mexico, you'll need to call our international ticket number," the agent informed the caller.

"No, I said New Mexico, not Mexico!"

The ticket agent paused, then retorted, "I don't care if you're from New Mexico or Old Mexico; if you're not American, you must call our international number!"

Funny. Maybe.

Not long ago, the Gallup Company surveyed college students around the globe on geographic knowledge. Unsurprisingly, U.S. college students brought up the rear. Twenty-five percent could not identify the Pacific Ocean on a map of the world. One in three could not use a map to determine direction or calculate distance. One fourth could not name any NATO country. And one out of seven, when looking at a map of the world, could not find the good ole US of A. They did so poorly the Gallup Company labeled them "geographically illiterate."[8]

It's time to think globally. It's time to go globally. It's time to live globally.

A DIFFERENT KIND OF CHRISTIAN

My brothers and I had traveled to the western edge of Zimbabwe to raft the Zambezi River. We boarded our raft at the base of the Victoria Falls. Massive amounts of water spilled over the top of the giant falls and dropped almost a thousand feet; the roar was deafening. The falls are the largest in the world, more than a mile wide and over three hundred feet high. Mist from the spray that fills the air like fog can be seen for fifty miles; the locals call it "smoke that thunders." The water from the falls rushes down the gorge in torrents, creating the world's largest rapids. In the United States, the highest-class rapid you are allowed to raft is a Class 5. The Zambezi's white-water rapids can top 7 and 8. Here's what I read later about white-water classes: "Completion of a Class 6 rapid without serious injury or death is widely considered to be a matter of luck or extreme skill." Great.

As I sat on the edge of the eight-person raft, all suited up in a tight, overstuffed life jacket and a thick crash helmet, I felt like an overcautious tourist about to mount an underpowered moped in Honolulu or rent roller-blades on Huntington Beach. The Zambezi couldn't be that dangerous, could it?

But then our guide caused me to begin questioning my logic. His first words were, "When the raft flips ..." There was no "If the raft flips," or "On the off chance we get flipped," but "When the raft flips." He went on, "... stay in the rough water. You will be tempted to swim toward the stagnant water at the edge of the banks. Don't do it. Because it is in the stagnant water that the crocs wait for you. They are large and hungry. Even when the raft flips, stay in the rough water."

Stagnancy will kill your spirit. The Christian who is not being used by God to change lives, to make a difference for Christ, will dry up, stagnate. Transformation will not happen.

Are you restless? Is your routine boring you mad? Do you sense that you should be doing much more with your life than you are today? For most, I am almost certain the answer is *yes*. The Bible tells us that God puts this dissatisfaction with a stagnant life in your heart.

God has a hard time working change in a life that is not going anywhere.

———

To finish the Zambezi story, the very first rapid we hit violently twisted our raft, folded it in half, and shot it in the air to land upside down. You bet I stayed in the rough water. After we pulled everyone back on board, our faithful guide started heading for the banks with the other rafts in our group. "Why are you stopping?" I asked.

"This is the chicken run; we stop here and let the chickens out to run." He was right—eighty dollars was not enough to keep about a dozen tourists from the other rafts in the white water risking their lives.

Many believers sense this restless heart but do nothing about it, usually because of fear. Fear is the cord Satan uses to bind our hands and hearts, keeping us self-justified in spiritual stagnancy. In his writings, Moses tells of bringing God's people to the banks of the Jordan River. He implored them to trust God and cross the river and take the land God had promised to them. They refused. They refused to go because the fear of what lay on the other side was greater than their passion for God. They feared the unknown, they were terrified of giant-sized opposition, and they were scared of failure.

Forty years later, Joshua led the Israelites into the raging waters of a flooded Jordan River and to the life-transforming experience of trusting God to work on their behalf. They became a changed nation, new people—people full of faith.

The missional church of tomorrow will be global in its purpose and function—not afraid to stop feeding its own church machine in order to change a broken world. Not afraid to get out of the boat to do things locally and globally that make its people uncomfortable.

My brothers and I stayed in the raft that day. Our raft must have flipped four more times. We were tossed like rag dolls and left in the river to battle the crocodiles. But we stayed in the white water. Yes, there were moments when I thought I would die, but I wouldn't trade that Zambezi thrill ride for anything.

The church of tomorrow must resist stagnancy. God needs us out there in the rough waters, pouring our lives into people.

We can't be still—we can't be silent anymore.

The life following hard after God is so much more exhilarating than many have allowed. Let's become like the revolutionaries of the early church. God has an unparalleled adventure waiting for you. There's purpose, there's danger, there's transformation for all who step out.

Live that way. Live in the white water. Live where it's just a little bit uncertain and unsafe. Live where something thrilling just might change you forever.

It's time to live differently.

Ideas for Becoming the Expatriate

If you are a student, sign up for a study-abroad program and spend a semester or year studying in a foreign country.

PART II

CONFLICT DIAMONDS

Love the Lord your God with all your mind.

Twonga's life in hell began ten years ago. The Lord's Resistance Army (LRA) rebels needed fresh recruits, so in the dead of night they attacked her village. The young rebel soldiers killed any men who resisted or attempted to escape. They rounded up all the young boys and young women to conscript them into their guerrilla army.

My brother Paul, who was living in Uganda at the time, listened to Twonga's story with a team of trauma counselors whom he had escorted to the gritty northern Ugandan town of Gulu.

For more than ten years, Joseph Kony had been trying to lead a rebellion against the Ugandan government from across the border in Sudan. In constant short supply of fighters, he would raid villages in Uganda and abduct children, the easiest targets, forcing them to become child soldiers.

Twonga, twelve years old, was marched back to the rebel base and forced to sit on the floor of a cramped room with dozens of other newly abducted children. The rebel commander stormed in and said, "Tonight you will all become killers. Tonight you will all learn to shed blood. And once you are a killer, your people back in your village will never want you home."

I tell you what happened next because it is true; if it shocks and disturbs you, then you're like me. On nights when I think about Twonga's story, I sometimes wish I did not know it myself. But this world is littered with places of hell on earth, and if we have any hope of changing that, we cannot close our eyes and ears to what happens. We simply cannot.

The commander then tossed a single piece of paper high in the air. The paper floated weightlessly down and landed silently on the legs of one of the girls sitting on the floor. The commander then ordered her to her feet. "To become killers tonight, I want all of you to kill this girl—you must bite her to death! Your teeth are your weapon. If you refuse, we will kill you next."

Twonga began to sob. "I cannot get the small girl's face out of my head. I still wake up from nightmares, sweating and crying because I dream about this awful night over and over. I cannot get her face out of my head."

CHAPTER 3

PLACES OF HELL

If there is a place in this world where children are forced to bite one another to death, that is a place of hell on earth.

Rob Bell writes about two universes—heaven and hell. And these domains are not just future places of hope or dread; they are present realities.[1]

God, in His wonderful way, lets us touch heaven. Being in love is a taste of heaven. Enjoying music with friends is a bit of heaven. Forgiveness, grace, generosity, babies, sandy beaches, hot Krispy Kreme doughnuts, art, flowers, and just about anything beautiful are pieces of heaven. The beauty and joy of heaven are all around.

In the same way, we see the bitterness of hell clear and present in this world: hate, abuse, addictions, racism, rape, bigotry, prejudice, poverty, and suffering.

The point here is that if places of hell really do exist, then by all means, God's people must be about the business of taking a piece of heaven to them.

HELL

"Welcome to hell," the European doctor greeted our medical team snidely at the entrance to the Lilongwe Hospital. Hell is what it was.

I had first visited hell a few years earlier when Boyd, a young man I knew in Lilongwe, was struck by a car while crossing the road at dusk.

Boyd's father showed up at my house in the dark and asked anxiously if I would drive him and his family to the hospital to find his son.

The stench was nauseating. Every part of the hospital was in some state of disrepair. Nothing appeared to have been painted in years. I watched the staff mop floors that remained curiously grimy.

We found Boyd on a dingy gurney in the hallway leading to the ER. He had a compound fracture; the bone protruded through the skin. His leg, his pants, and the gurney were all drenched in blood. He was still bleeding.

"Has he seen a doctor?" I asked.

An ER attendant spoke. "No, we are waiting for the doctor."

I walked into the ER to try to find help. There were no doctors, so I rounded up two interns and convinced them to bring Boyd into the ER to get the bleeding stopped and clean the puncture wound in his leg. They agreed, rolled him into the ER, and promised to look after him until the doctor arrived. I felt good about being helpful and headed home.

That was Friday night. Late Monday evening, Boyd's father was back at my door. "Boyd is in a lot of pain. Could you help me with some money for some pain medication?"

"Pain medication?" I was surprised. "Once a fracture is set, there should be no pain."

"The leg has not been set yet," his father replied.

What? Boyd lay there in the hospital for three days with a compound fracture, and no one had set it! I knew the orthopedic surgeon would not be in at night, so I waited until the morning and headed back to "hell" with several of my Malawian college students. We hunted the halls for an hour looking for the one orthopedic surgeon in the country and finally found him in an operating theater, teaching a class. He waved me in, and I told him about Boyd. He was unaware of the case and graciously told me to bring him.

We found Boyd, but none of the nurses could find a gurney to roll him to the operating room. So we picked up his bed, each taking a corner, and we carried him to the operating theater.

His leg had rotted. It took almost six months to heal.

If there's a place in this world where people lie for days with gaping wounds—that's a place of hell on earth.

———

I've heard of people in Malawi eating dirt during the dry season when the crops are dead and their supplies have expired. They say it takes away the hunger pangs.

I had a difficult time fathoming this until I saw a news story a month ago on mothers in Haiti who made cookies out of mud for their children. With no money and no food in the home, the mothers say at least it relieves the pain in their children's stomachs.

> If there is a place in this world where mothers have to make cookies out of mud ... that's a place of hell on earth.

> If young men are lying in hospital beds in Africa with broken legs because they have no money to pay a bribe ... that's a place of hell on earth.

> If women are being sold as sex slaves in Ethiopia ... that's a place of hell on earth.

> If infants are dying of malaria, a completely curable disease, in Zambia ... that's a place of hell on earth.

> If women are being stoned to death for adultery in Sudan ... that's a place of hell on earth.

> If children in Uganda are being stolen from their beds to be made into child soldiers ... that's a place of hell on earth.

BOTHERED

I'll be honest. I write all of this with the intention of bothering you. I hope that you will no longer be willing to ignore people who hurt.

Oppression, injustice, poverty, bigotry, and abuse are real and present. But it doesn't have to be this way. God put you and me here to make this world a better place, a more beautiful place. When Jesus left, He asked that you and I continue to change and love the world. The mission and purpose of the local church was never intended to end at the edge of our community.

King Solomon writes about the heart of God: "Rescue the perishing; don't hesitate to step in and help. If you say, 'Hey, that's none of my business,' will that get you off the hook? Someone is watching you closely, you know—Someone not impressed with weak excuses."[2]

So whatever the cost, go in the name of Jesus and love people who hurt. Tell them and show them that God has a better way, a more beautiful way, a life-giving way.

CONFLICT

Educators have discovered an interesting phenomenon: We learn best and comprehend more when our minds are disturbed. In other words, the more people are bothered by what they are being taught—because it is new or radically different and they disagree—then the more likely the information will change the way they think and live. The process of wrestling with difficult concepts makes them better thinkers and ultimately deeper people. The process even has a name—cognitive conflict (or disequilibration).

Jesus was brilliant at this. He masterfully used parables or illustrations to disturb those He taught. When the intellect Nicodemus found Him at night and asked Him to explain the Way, Jesus said,

"You'll need to be born again." Nicodemus said, "What? How can that happen?" But Jesus explained further until Nicodemus finally got it and believed.[3]

The young, wealthy executive who asked Jesus how to get to heaven never did get it. So he walked away—frustrated and sad.

The truths Jesus taught were so disturbing that some people became infuriated. The first time He taught in Nazareth, He said, "I'm the Messiah—but I'm not here to battle the Romans. And by the way, God is for everyone—not just the Jews."[4]

They tried to throw Him over a cliff.

The Jews thought the teachings of this so-called messiah were absurd! But wasn't it the absurd nature of Jesus' teaching that made His words so powerful? Black is white, and white is black. Up is down, and down is up. When the Romans slap you in the street, turn and let them do it again. Love people who don't like you. Meekness is powerful. You win when you come in last. Value people of every race. Give more to others, and keep less for yourself.

The way of the Christ is no ordinary way. To follow Him, you have to think differently, and you have to live differently. But His way of thinking will change you forever! His ideas are not just life changing; they are life-giving.

Being disturbed is not just a good way to learn—it's necessary for transformation.

Jesus crafted the stories He told to have this effect. He often would talk about an idea people knew well, such as the Old Testament principle of revenge—an eye for an eye—then He would throw out a new way of thinking about revenge and crumble an age-old policy. He would always propose equilibration to their thinking by offering

a better way to live, a more beautiful way to live, a
to live. But He let them choose.

DIAMONDS

Spiritual transformation often happens in the moments of life that stun us. When we experience, watch, or hear of something disturbing, it creates this *cognitive conflict* that can change the way we think and live.

You may already know how diamonds are formed. Carbon, which is just black dirt, is compressed by millions of pounds of pressure by the earth's weight. This extreme pressure and heat from the earth's core transform the carbon into something pure and beautiful. The greater the heat and pressure, the more pure (or clear) the diamond forms.

In much the same way, I'm convinced we are transformed through moments of spiritual conflict. Under the pressure of going globally and giving our lives away, we open ourselves to the possibility of God crafting something beautiful in our souls. He uses the pressure of the experience and the heat of the moment—sometimes literally—to transform us spiritually and make our lives a bit more beautiful.

We have two options. We can choose to stay and ignore. Or we can choose to go and see and be disturbed. One choice leads to a kind of death; the other leads to life and change and hope.

THE TRANSFORMING EXPERIENCE

Few experiences are as effective in disturbing the way we think as the global one, whether through serving, loving, or showing compassion.

I watch college students and adults every year struggle to assimilate what they experience and learn when they leave home and give their lives away.

In East Africa, for example, I've seen college students who travel with me struggle to accept the level of absolute destitute poverty that exists. They say things like, "There is no way the government has set the minimum wage at thirty cents A DAY! You must mean an hour." Or, "You can't be serious that this family cannot afford to buy a ten-dollar mosquito net for their new baby." Or, "Fifty percent of high schoolers in urban areas are HIV positive? That's impossible."

Really?

The goal of Christian education is unique. Our objective is not simply to transfer information from teacher to student, but rather to change lives. Jesus taught in order to forever change the way His hearers lived. And so Jesus' teaching moved them beyond *knowing* content to living transformed lives.

I studied under Ted Ward at Trinity Divinity School. Ted, an influential constructive critic of Christian education for the past four decades, is a leading proponent of nonformal educational methods. He explains that experience promotes intellectual growth; in other words, we learn through our experiences. The process is termed *experiential learning* or *nonformal education*.[5]

For centuries, academia, often disconnected from the practical concerns of the world, represented education as solely taking place on the university campus and in the classroom. In many cases, this is the diligent professor dutifully standing before a captive audience of nineteen-year-olds, lecturing emotionlessly from dog-eared notes. In recent years, however, this stale mode of transferring information has been challenged as educators better understand cognitive development. Most important, people are beginning to realize that learners best retain and understand information—and are transformed—when the learning is experiential.

My point in explaining concepts like *disequalibration* and *nonformal learning* is to demonstrate the truth that global experiences change the way we think and live. They enlarge our idea of God and expand the impact of our lives. Our epistemology (how we know) is reoriented, and we have a new worldview and a new view of what God can do through us.

JOLT

My first pastoral position following college was as a junior high pastor. I loved every minute, really. Once a month on a Wednesday night I had Jolt Cola night. In case you don't know, Jolt Cola cans read: "Twice the caffeine and all the sugar of the leading soft drink." By the end of the night, kids were bouncing off the walls … literally. Their parents loved me. My first retreat that winter, twenty-one kids accepted Christ. I sometimes wonder if the cola helped open their eyes.

Sometimes we need a *jolt* spiritually. The Bible is filled with such examples. Moses was wandering the deserts of life when God stunned him and spoke from a burning bush. Jonah had to spend three dark nights in the gut of a giant fish before he would let God lead his life. Hosea had to suffer the pain of watching his wife sell her body as a prostitute so that God could change the nation of

Israel. The ancient prophet Joel was changed in Babylonian captivity. Peter the Christ-follower was carelessly committed to his Rabbi until he witnessed His tortured death on a cross. But afterwards he wept. He changed. He became a pioneering missionary, church planter, leader … and martyr. He was transformed. And the list could go on.

CONFLICT DIAMONDS

The wars for diamonds are not fought in Tulsa, Tacoma, or Tupelo. The conflicts over diamonds are waged in the African swamps of Sierra Leone, the jungles of Liberia, and the deserts of Angola.

Similarly, if Christians today want to live open to the possibility of dramatic spiritual transformation, then we must *go*. Go where life is a bit more tested and trying.

I would like to tell you about Holly, a college student from Tempe. When Holly traveled to Africa, she spent her first day in a Malawian village treating sick children. Late in the day a desperate mother rushed to the front of the line, holding her listless infant. The baby's name was Grace; AIDS had ravaged her tiny body. Holly's mother, an RN, held the baby on the bus all the way back to the city and to the hospital. Early the next morning, Holly and others on the team rushed to the malnutrition ward in hopes of seeing that the little girl had improved. Grace had not lived through the night.

Hearing Holly's story probably causes you to feel some degree of empathy. But now imagine *you* holding the same child, in the same dusty village of Chiuza, *you* sitting on the same bus, then anxiously rushing to the hospital in the morning to see if *your* tiny patient was still breathing. Wouldn't you agree that the emotional conflict and moral tension you experience would be far more real?

Transformation does not happen sitting in front of the TV; it doesn't happen sitting in Starbucks, sitting in a classroom, or even sitting in a pew. A critical ingredient in the transformation process is *experience*.

Holly now says she's going to medical school so that she can return to Africa and help heal tiny, sick babies.

Ideas for Becoming the Expatriate

Sponsor a child and get to know him or her.
Children of the Nations (COTNI.org) or World Vision
(WorldVision.org) are great places to start.

CHAPTER 4

DISTURBED

I invited Bo and Pat out for Mongolian barbecue last week because I was intrigued by the new agency they had created. Pat said, "We've started Branded-PHX to end the sexual exploitation of girls and young women in the greater Phoenix area. It's happening right here in our suburbs. We're appalled, and we plan to end it." And they are. Two guys, leading the charge to free countless young girls in a city of millions.

Then Bo went on to tell me what he and the international aid organization he works for are doing in Africa. "Right now we are treating the entire population of Burundi for parasites."

"Really?" I asked, surprised. "That's about nine million people!"

"Yes," Bo answered matter-of-factly. "That's what the

president of Burundi has requested, so that's what we're doing—right now."

Audacious but amazing.

Two men—changing the world for good. I hope I can live that way.

———◆———

What is the most important thing about you?

You may answer, *my career, my education, my family, my house, my savings, my good looks*. I venture to say no, it is none of these.

I've heard it said like this: The most important thing about you is *what your thoughts are when you think about God!*[1]

What fills your mind when you think about God? What idea do you have of Him? Is He enormous, grand, and infinite? Do you feel tiny in comparison to His vastness? Are you in wonder and awe? Do you sense great mystery in trying to understand the incomprehendable?[2]

When you give your life away, particularly in a global setting, you see God in the right size. You realize God is not trapped in a cul-de-sac. God is not limited. You discover a right idea of God, an idea of Him that is unbelievably large. You will find the God of Scripture: King of Kings, Mighty One, Alpha and Omega, Creator, All-sufficient One, All-powerful One, One and Only! A right idea of God is spectacular.

Give your life away. Go and let God fill you with wonder. He is so much bigger than you've ever imagined.

———◆———

I have been a basketball junkie my entire life. I played all through high school but was far from talented enough make the squad at Biola University. But that never kept my friends and me from thinking we were an international basketball force. Every winter and summer break throughout college, we would return to West Africa with borrowed nicknames on the backs of our jerseys: Magic, Dr. J, Iceman, and Chocolate Thunder. We would then drive across Liberia and the Ivory Coast, looking to dominate any high school or club basketball team we could find.

So as a college pastor in Wheaton, when I wrote the Cuban Basketball Federation asking permission to bring a team of college basketball players to tour their country, I felt confident that my international experience would carry our team.

More than a month passed with no reply, and I assumed my letter had been discarded and considered insignificant. But then a fax came with a warm invitation for us to come to Cuba; it was signed by the president of the Cuban Basketball Federation.

I excitedly announced to our college ministry of about two hundred students that we would be going to Cuba on a basketball sports-ministry trip, and I needed players! Two weeks later, at our first meeting, I had twenty-one students in a circle, all excited about the trip. But as we went around the circle and they shared their basketball experience, I realized I only had one baller.

A week later I was scheduled to go before our board of elders and present the trip, but I still did not have a team. The night before the meeting, I tossed in bed until two in the morning, pleading with God to give me a team before my meeting—honestly, it was more a prayer of desperation than hope. So I was completely surprised the next morning when Chris Bonga, one of our college students who was away at school and a basketball stud, called and said, "Palmer, my roommate and I want to play on your team going to Cuba, and we each have a friend who wants to play as well." That was five players! I had a team. I was amazed at God's quick response to my lame prayer.

Less than a week later, I received a follow-up fax from the Cuban Basketball Federation with the schedule of our games in Cuba. I had to sit down; my knees were weak. Included in our itinerary were three games in three different cities … playing the Cuban Olympic Team!

I was completely discouraged as I thought about my five gym-rats going up against a country's national team. I needed more players, and I needed bigger players. Fast.

I went back to God and began to plead, "God, give me two guys six feet six inches—that's all I ask." For some reason I thought two players six feet six would help us be respectable.

The very next morning—I'm serious—just before noon, two big guys walked into my office. They were buddies, one from Taylor University and one from Wheaton College, and they said, "Palmer, we're here to ask if we can play basketball in Cuba with you."

I was thrilled. But I had to ask, "How tall are you guys?"

Bill answered matter-of-factly, "Six feet, six inches," and Doug followed, "Six-six."

"Just checking," I answered. "We'll make room."

I was on top of the world. God was good. God was big. And I told everyone who would listen how excited I was about the team I was taking to Cuba and how God had given me two six-foot-six players to carry us on their backs.

Surprisingly, as I talked to people who really knew international basketball, they all questioned the adequacy of my team. One coach out of Texas in particular, who had traveled to Cuba with his basketball team, said, "Are you serious? Your center is six-six? You're gonna get killed; their guards are six-six, their centers are over seven feet."

After a couple of weeks of this kind of encouraging feedback, I felt like I had to go back to God. This time I prayed, "God, one more time, I just need two players six feet eight." That's NBA star LeBron James's size. I thought if I had two horses LeBron's size, then we'd be in business.

Time was running out. I gave God a week.

I called every sports ministry and Christian college I could think of but kept striking out. The final day came and went ... and still nothing. I was defeated, discouraged, and down. "I can't do the trip," I told myself. "That's it, we're done."

As I got ready for bed that night at about nine, my phone rang; on the other end was a college baller from Biola who had heard about our trip and wanted to go with us to Cuba.

I was glad to have the extra body, but I was looking for height. "How tall are you?" I asked.

"Six-eight," he answered. Of course he was. I should have known.

Less than an hour later, my phone rang again. Before he could say anything more than "My name is Kyle, and I'm calling about Cuba," I asked, "You're not six-eight, are you?"

His only response was, "How in the world did you know?"

I'm not kidding you. That's how it went that night.

At 11:00 p.m. my phone rang one more time. One more player ready to go to Cuba. This guy played Division I and was six feet eleven! I hadn't even dreamed of asking for a center that large. But I think God wanted to settle once and for all that He was bigger than my greatest request. He was larger than my greatest obstacle. He was sufficient for every need. He was more than I ever wanted.

How big was God now? He wanted to ice the cake.

CUL-DE-SACS

When you go global and give your life away, you expand your idea of God.

Over my years as a pastor, I've often heard people pray. I'm sometimes surprised by the trite nature of our prayers. I hear people pray for sick pets, aching backs, and better weather. Disturbing questions meander through my head (of course, pastors are supposed to be nice guys, so I can't always verbalize what I think): *Is your God really that small? Is that all you want to ask of Him or want Him to do through your life?" I want to shout, "God can do much more than that! He doesn't live at the end of your street.*

I'm convinced many people worship a cul-de-sac God. They picture Him living at the end of their street, doing nice little things for them.

But this is not the size of the God of the Bible. Go, and let God show you His true size. Give your life away and have your idea of God radically altered.

I believe part of the problem is that many Christians are not raised to think deeply about God and their faith. One of my Trinity professors used to share a revealing story about Christian thinking: A third grade Sunday school teacher said to her class, "I'm thinking of something that's gray, climbs in trees, has a bushy tail, and collects acorns for the winter. Can you tell me what I'm thinking about?"

Cautiously, one boy raised his hand and ventured, "It sure sounds like a squirrel, but I know the answer is supposed to be … Jesus!"

Unfortunately, we sometimes grow up like that. Not thinking deeply about our faith, we recite pat answers and give shallow insight. The Bible, however, invites meaningful study and contemplation. We must become a thinking people.

AMBITIONS

Abandon your small ambitions. God is bigger than them.

Not long ago, I was listening to a speaker at a national pastors conference and couldn't believe what I heard as his proposition: *Shrink Your World*. Really? Are you kidding me? He went on to explain, "Too many of us allow our lives to be too spread out. A few years ago my family and I committed to shrink our world to a five-mile perimeter. Our grocery shopping, haircuts, soccer leagues, schools, work, and church would all be contained in a five-mile radius. We have succeeded. We've now made a new resolution: to shrink our world to a one-mile radius." This was his message. This was his challenge to pastors from across the country. Shrink!

He even found a Christian publisher to print this novel concept.

Absurd. Nowhere in Scripture are we instructed to shrink our world. Let people who have no concept of a living, omnipotent God shrink their world.

Christ's call is to GO! Go large, go far, go where no one has gone before. I love the words of the ancient prophet Isaiah: "Enlarge the place of your tent, stretch your tent curtains wide, do not hold back; lengthen your cords, strengthen your stakes. For you will spread out to the right and to the left."[3]

The quiet plea from those who worship in the cul-de-sac is, "Do less, stay close, cut the costs, reduce the risks." You don't have to listen. You don't have to listen.

MUY GRANDE

Jesus reminds us to have a big idea of God because His plans for us are unusually large: "Bear much fruit." Not simply bear fruit, or do pretty well at bearing fruit, but definitively "much fruit."[4]

I was in the home of Cuban Pastor Elmer Lavastida when he asked if I would like a *naranja* (orange).

"Sure," I told him.

He reached down behind his kitchen counter and with two hands lifted up a piece of fruit the size of a volleyball.

"That's an orange?" I asked. "Are you serious?" He told me that's how they grow in Cuba.

Now that's "much fruit." The *naranja-muy-grande* life is the life God wants for you. It's larger than you ever believed possible.

THE SALAD YEARS

I sometimes wonder whose God is big enough to take them to the places of hell on earth.

I think I know. I believe I've put my finger on a certain demographic that will go at any cost.

There is a time in this life when we are bothered by injustice and moral wrong more than at any other time. There is a time in this life when we live with practically no fear. There's a time in this life when we are willing to try just about anything—and we do. That time in our lives is the young adult years—the university years—the salad years. Developmental psychologists refer to these years as *the critical years*.

One hot spring afternoon when I was a student at Biola, I grabbed my towel and headed to the pool, which was ringed with California girls I was convinced needed to know my name. So I decided to do something to catch their attention. Believing an impressive dive off the three-meter board would spark their interest, I headed up the ten-foot-high platform, went out to the end, and gave the board a good snap. The audience of bikini-clad women began to take notice; something dramatic was about to happen.

I had grown up diving off a three-meter board and could pull off several difficult one-and-a-halfs, but for some reason on this day I thought a gainer would be the most impressive. I had never attempted a gainer.

I paused like an Olympic diver, long enough for every young female present to look up, then sprinted, took a huge bounce and leaned back. I had seen guys pull off a gainer plenty of times and it looked pretty easy—just lean back, spread eagle, then straighten out and enter the water like Greg Louganis. But I quickly realized that when I leaned back all I did was put myself parallel to the water.

Everything I had learned in ninth grade physics whirled through my mind—*how do I increase my rotation!? Mass times velocity equals ... something!?*

I remained calm at first, I tried leaning back more, then started moving my arms, then my legs began to move; nothing, still parallel to the water. With every appendage now flailing wildly, like a baboon falling from a tree I slammed into the water, flat on my back.

The thunderous clap was so loud the lifeguard was certain something bad had happened. *She* blew her whistle and dove in after me.

I made it out of the pool, picked up my towel, and headed back to my dorm.

Here's the thing about diving—you can't change direction in midair! Everything you do in the dive is determined by your launch off the board. The motion you begin on the diving board is the motion you will continue in the air.

Life is kind of like that. The most important things we do with our lives are often determined by the choices we make, the values we form, the decisions we follow, the affections we develop, the allegiances we create *during the critical years.*

Wheaton College students affectionately refer to these years as the "salad years." Because in many ways, they are the best years. In the salad years, you hold life by the tail. The world is yours for the taking. The doors are all open. You may live in any city you choose. You can take any career path you like. You can marry whoever you like … well, not really—but you get my point.

So much of who we are later in life is defined in those few developmentally important years. Think about your parents for a moment and the music they listen to. I can bet money it's not Lil Wayne or Usher. Your mom's still playing Michael Bolton, and your dad's waiting for Kiss's reunion tour.

In *The Critical Years,* a seminal work on this formative life stage, Sharon Parks writes about the motion of faith.[5] She argues that this period is a unique and identifiable developmental stage, one not recognized by Fowler or Piaget.

These years are precious. Much of who we are spiritually is shaped in these years. A stimulating environment and new opportunities will promote spiritual growth and transformation. Conversely, a stagnant environment and negative conditions will slow or even block spiritual development.

Possibly the most valuable aspect of the salad years is that they are the years when we dream dreams. Parks writes, "The young adult soul can be beckoned beyond the conventional, the mundane, and the assumed, to invest in the promise of all life."[6]

Extreme sports are popular with the college-age crowd for a reason. Your thirtysomethings with the soccer leagues, Suburbans, and BlackBerrys are not the ones jumping off bridges and out of airplanes. A longing for adventure, a willingness to risk, a desire to make what is wrong right innately reside in the soul of the young adult.

I write about the critical years because if that is where you find yourself, then value them. Don't waste a day. I write about the critical years because parents and leaders and pastors and educators need to recognize the unique value of those around us who live in these years. Listen to them, include them, promote them, treasure them, encourage them, equip them, and learn from them—because they are filled with potential.

Even if you're not a twentysomething, you can still live that way. You don't have to be so cautious, you don't have to only do what you've done before, and you don't have to plan so far ahead.

Start living with the spontaneity of a twenty-year-old. I'm increasingly alarmed by how far out people plan. I have friends who reserve campsites by the beach a year ahead. Who knows what they're doing a year from now? On my way out of the dentist office the receptionist wanted to schedule me for a cleaning. She gave me a date and a time six months into the future—and then asked if I wanted to write it down. I politely said, "No, call me the day before. If I'm still around I'll be glad to stop in." I have no idea where I'll be or what I'll be doing at one in the afternoon six months from today! I grew up in Africa; when it's Monday nobody's really sure what they're doing on Wednesday. I believe life works better that way.

Those in the critical years live like that. A few years ago I was moving from Wheaton to Phoenix to help start a church. I didn't want to do it alone. Dan, a college student and radio DJ, happened to be riding with me when I was processing the move, so I said, "Hey, how about moving to Arizona with me to help me start a church?"

"Sure."

That was it. No questions. No drama. Life's easy. Plus it was winter in Chicago.

The university-aged are also uniquely motivated to change this world for good: "A central strength of the young adult is the capacity to respond to visions of the world as it might become. This is the time in every generation for renewal of the human vision."[7]

This unique impetus was the force behind the great student volunteer movement of the late nineteenth century, the One Day movement of the midnineties, and the recent student revolution in Iran. Young adults see life as less complicated than older adults do. What must be done appears clear. To them, anything and everything is possible.

While at Harvard, Lawrence Kohlberg once taught a course on moral choice. Carol Gilligan studied the effect the course had on the student's moral reasoning. Gilligan's fundamental finding is that young adults sense a deep "obligation to relieve human misery and suffering if possible."[8]

This is why Jason Russell, Bobby Bailey, and Laren Poole founded Invisible Children. These three aspiring filmmakers traveled to northern Uganda in their early twenties because they were disturbed by the atrocities taking place in Dafur, Sudan.

While looking for a way across the border they found themselves in the middle of a human tragedy. Thousands of children who feared being abducted by the LRA to fight as child soldiers were walking miles and miles every night from their rural villages to seek refuge in the towns of Gulu and Lira. The concrete floors of bus depots and hospital basements became their beds.

The three friends couldn't believe what they were witnessing: literally, a flood of children filling the towns every night. Why hadn't anyone told them? Why was the world silent?

They began to film the atrocity, produced a documentary, founded an organization, met with government officials, and called the world's attention to the tragedy in northern Uganda. Individuals, churches, schools, and governments have responded. The tide has turned. Joseph Kony is on the run. Children near Gulu are again sleeping in their own beds at night.

Do you see how it's often people in the critical years, like Jason and Bobby and Laren, who are leading the charge to rescue children like Twonga from places of hell on earth?

STARS

In most suburban communities, light pollution and smog dim our view of the stars. Maybe that's one of the reasons our God is too small.

A word was added to the dictionary of standard American English this year: *ginormous*. I think Christians should claim it as the best descriptor of God.

Trying to understand the God-sized life He wants you to live is like trying to study astronomy without ever leaving the classroom. Tonight I invite you to get out of town, away from the fog of light and noise. Go to the beach, climb a hill, drive out to the desert, hike into the woods ... then just sit and stare deep into the night sky. Rediscover the intriguing, vast beauty of God's creation and reclaim a huge idea of God.

———

When you go global and give your life away, you will see the world differently. You will understand why cul-de-sacs can't contain God. You will see God like you've never seen Him before—wonderfully ginormous.

That is a right idea of God.

Ideas for Becoming the Expatriate

Study a new language, then travel to a place where you can speak it!

PART III

DO WORK

Love the Lord your God with all your strength.

I pulled up to the gritty city dump outside of Tijuana with thirty-plus junior highers in our church van. The funk of garbage was mixed with the lingering smell of smoke from the hundreds of small fires that burned deep inside the piles of refuse. This was the first missions trip I had led with this age group, and for practically all of them, it was their first time to leave America. As we pulled into the middle of the grim scene, my van full of unruly thirteen-year-olds went oddly silent.

They are known as *pickers*: hundreds of boys and girls as young as five and six years old working alongside their parents, rummaging for scrap that can be resold. Digging through the smoldering mountain of garbage makes the entire livelihood of these families. On our visit, adults with children in tow were scattered across the piles of steamy refuse; faces dull and void of life, they dug for hours. The children's clothes were torn and filthy, their hands and feet black from the soot and grime.

As we climbed out of the van, the nauseating stench made me pause. But without hesitation, seemingly oblivious to the mess all around, the junior high boys fanned out and invited the children over for soccer and kickball. The girls began a line of children outside a small, temporary shelter; here they spent the day giving baths, dressing the children in new clothes we brought with us, then combing their beautiful, dark hair to a shine.

As the sun began to set, we loaded up to head back across the border. Soon after leaving I noticed one of our girls' shoulders heaving as she sobbed silently. I turned and asked, "What's wrong?"

Her answer was soft. "It's the kids. I feel so bad about the kids who live in the dump."

"But it's been a good day," I said. "We washed a lot of kids today. You left them clean and beautiful. You did so well."

"I know," she whispered tearfully, "but who will wash them tomorrow?"

CHAPTER 5

PIECES OF HEAVEN

This was Kim's first day in the village of Mtziliza, and within minutes of arriving, a two-year-old girl wandered up to her with arms outstretched. Kim picked her up and held her tight.

Three teams totaling fifty-four people traveled from our church to Africa with me last summer; one team to Uganda, one to Liberia, and one to Malawi. Part of our Malawi team's job was to simply love orphans of AIDS. And that's what Kim was determined to do.

The toddler laid her head on Kim's shoulder and within minutes was asleep. As Kim, a twentysomething art teacher, held her close, she asked about the child. Both parents had died of AIDS; her six-year-old sister was her sole caretaker. The girls slept at night on the floor of a relative's home that was crowded with dozens of other children in the same plight.

For more than two hours Kim held the sleeping child. Her back ached terribly as she had nowhere to sit, but Kim said there was no way she was going to lay the sleeping orphan down in the dirt. So she just held on.

PIECES OF HEAVEN

When you enter the grime of a city dump to wash children, you take a piece of heaven with you.

When you hold a child orphaned by AIDS until she falls asleep in your comforting arms, you take a piece of heaven.

When you take a mosquito net to the hut of an African family, you take a piece of heaven.

When you give a barefoot man a pair of shoes, you give a piece of heaven.

When you buy groceries for a family whose father has lost his job, you give a piece of heaven.

God's people are at their best when they're giving themselves away.

I believe Jesus wanted more than anything else for His followers to make this world a little bit more beautiful, to share a little bit more of His love, and to take a piece of heaven to places of hell on earth.

If places of hell exist, then in the name of Jesus, take a piece of heaven there.

DO WORK

Okay, so I sometimes watch *Rob and Big* with my sons, and the characters make me laugh. Judge me if you must. If you've watched the show, you know Big will often say to Rob, "It's time to *do work, son.*"

Christian spirituality has a clear *doing* component. (I think Big would like that.) There's work to be done. Do the work of the cross. We have a moral duty to physically respond to the needs of hurting people around us.

Jesus made this so clear in His parables, the most poignant of which is the well-known story of the good Samaritan. Frustrated by the hypocrisy of the religious leaders, Jesus challenges those listening to stop acting so religious and begin *doing* this thing called love.

What I'm trying to communicate here is that faith does not only happen in the mind and the soul. It's not enough to say, "I know God." Or even, "I love God with all my heart." Those are necessary and good, but if they are true, then we will *do* the love He calls us to.

Jesus' brother James says it well:

> *What good is it … if a man claims to have*
> *faith but has no deeds? Can such faith save*
> *him? Suppose a brother or sister is without*
> *clothes and daily food. If one of you says*
> *to him, "Go, I wish you well; keep warm*
> *and well fed," but does nothing about his*

physical needs, what good is it? In the same
way, faith by itself, if it is not accompanied
by action, is dead. But someone will say,
"You have faith; I have deeds." Show me
your faith without deeds, and I will show
you my faith by what I do.... You foolish
man ... faith without deeds is useless." [1]

James uses a stinging word in this passage. When he says you are foolish, he uses the Greek word *kenos*, which means "empty chatter." If you are not loving people who hurt, your religion's just a bunch of empty chatter. Period.

LOVE WORKS

Why does the church often wait for Hollywood to do love first? We can learn from men like Sean Penn, dubbed Captain America, who charged into the New Orleans floodwaters to rescue stranded people. The church can learn from people like Bono, a man who has committed his talents and resources to fighting AIDS in Africa.

We can follow the lead of women like Angelina Jolie and Madonna ... yes, even Madonna. These women have flown to Africa to love orphans and even take them home. How great a love is that, to raise an orphan as your own?

We can learn from emerging companies like LRG and Obey, who have grown a cult-army of teenagers who wear their products to remind the world that life is hell out there and we should live to make a difference. LRG's trademark is, "Adopt children not styles." Obey features T-shirts with pictures of African orphans that read, "Helping Other People Everywhere." We need to do the same.

Let's do the work of faith.

———

Katie Ponsness has started living this way. Katie, an ASU student at The Grove, stopped by my office just days before I was leaving with three teams for Africa. She handed me a hundred dollars she had earned from babysitting and said, "Could you do something for the kids in Africa?"

"Katie, this is generous!" I exclaimed. "How do you want me to use it?"

"You'll know," she said with a smile, and left.

A week later, our basketball team arrived at a Lilongwe high school to lead a clinic. I'd seen plenty of shoddy basketball courts in Africa, but this had to be the worst. Weeds grew up through the cracked asphalt. The backboards were made of pieces of one-by-six tied to a broken metal frame with electrical wire. The rims hung straight down and were useless. We spent the first hour trying to get duct tape to hold everything in place. Boards still slipped off the frame and crashed onto the court during our basketball clinic.

At the end of the afternoon, I pulled aside one of the school's graduates who had helped plan the event. "Doud, you're going to have to get the school to work on this court. You can't promote basketball with your court in this condition."

He said, "I've tried, but they won't give us money to fix it."

"How much do you think it would cost?" I asked.

He thought a moment. "Well, we would need to hire a welder to fix the frame. Then buy wood and hire a carpenter to rebuild the backboard. Maybe fifty dollars for each goal."

I remembered Katie's hundred dollars. "A college student from The Grove has sent you just enough," I told him with a smile.

I left him the money. About a month later, I received an email from Doud with pictures for Katie. His note read, "Both backboards and rims are up. We hired a welder and a carpenter. And we've cleaned the weeds and restriped the court. The students were so excited about having the court refurbished that they held a tournament that very day. We also wanted to thank Katie for her generous gift to our school, so we have named the court in her honor." And he attached a picture. Painted around the perimeter of the circle at center court were the words *The Katie Ponsness Basketball Court*.

Who's the blessed one now?

SIMPLY LIVE

I love golf and might play every day if I didn't have a wife, a job, and kids. I'm invited often by my friends to play because they know I love the game. But they know one thing about Palmer and golf—he won't play if it costs more than thirty-five dollars.

Jafalli, a laborer on the African Bible College campus, asked one day if he could sit down with me. He had a request. Jafalli explained that he owned some land in his village and wanted to build a house for his young family. He was renting a room for him and his wife, but they had just had their first baby and he wanted to build a home.

He asked if I would lend him the money to build the house. He promised to repay me, though it might take several years. But I was just a missionary professor at the time, not an investment banker. How would I be able to float this?

After listening to his need, I asked, "So how much are we talking about, Jafalli?"

"Two-thousand-five-hundred kwachas," he answered.

Two thousand five hundred? Hmmm. I did the exchange in my head, about seventy Malawian kwachas to the dollar. "You're asking for a home loan of thirty-five dollars?!"

"Yes."

"How can you build a house for that?"

"Well, it's not a big house. And the mud bricks are one kwacha each. Then I'll need about two or three bags of concrete for mortar. Then a few pieces of lumber to hold up the thatched roof, which I will cut and put on myself."

He really could build his mud-brick home for thirty-five dollars!

"Okay, Jafalli, then let's go with 10 percent down, and we'll amortize your loan over thirty years at 6.5 percent, making your payment twenty-eight kwachas a month."

No, I didn't say anything like that. And I didn't lend him the thirty-five dollars. I gave it to him.

I have such a difficult time spending thirty-five dollars on a passing pleasure when I know a family could have a house for that same amount. I don't know why the thought still bothers me. But it does.

If you have any aspirations at all of taking the love of God to hurting people, then please think about living just a little bit more simply.

We had a college student from our church spend a summer in Honduras. When she came home, she sat down with her parents and told them they needed to sell their home because it was too extravagant. It was large and beautiful, one of the nicest in Wheaton. She told them that after seeing the way people had to live in Honduras, she felt it was poor stewardship for her family to live in such opulence.

Her parents put the house on the market, sold it, and moved into a condo.

Not too many people will live that way.

LIVE LOVE

I'll try not to brag, but I'm proud of the people at The Grove, the church I'm privileged to pastor. I feel like they get it.

I recruited our Next Generation Ministries pastor from Guatemala. That's not where you normally go to look for student ministries pastors, but I liked his passion.

When Paul and his wife, Melinda, arrived, they brought with them a desire to help our people show the love of God to people in our community. To do this well, they founded a ministry called Live Love.

Our first Live Love project was to fill one hundred boxes with groceries and a turkey for Thanksgiving meals. We ran out of boxes before our second church service was over.

Next, the Live Love leaders met with our city officials and asked how we could serve the city. The officials asked if we would be willing to adopt and beautify a neglected neighborhood that had been hit with urban blight and crime. Live Love invited people from our church and the community to come on a Saturday to refurbish forty-six homes and yards.

The street was filled with hundreds of people. Teams of volunteers took on different houses. The fire department took a home; when I arrived, they were using their ladder truck to trim palm trees. Employees from Target even took on a house. All forty-six homes were made beautiful by the end of just one day.

Live Love recently ran another community work day for high school students. But here's the kicker—Paul told them there would be a ten-dollar cover charge to come serve! The money was used to buy mosquito nets for kids in Africa.

Over one hundred students showed up to work ... and paid the cover charge. The very next week, some of those very students were walking from hut to hut in Africa giving away a bit of heaven, a bit of themselves, and hundreds of mosquito nets.

Last summer, Paul and Melinda took a team of high schoolers to Malawi. While they were distributing mosquito nets in a rural village called Mgwayi, Paul asked the chief what they needed most. The chief said, "Clean water," and showed him a hole in a swamp where his people drew murky water.

On Paul's first Sunday back, he told the people of The Grove that we would be selling T-shirts that day that read in Chichewa (the Malawian language), *Live Love.* He said, "Whatever you pay today for a T-shirt will go toward digging a well for the Mgwayi village." Some people paid twenty dollars for one T-shirt. Some paid fifty. Some a hundred. And one person paid five thousand dollars for one T-shirt. Almost six thousand dollars in T-shirts were sold in just one day. We later received a bid to dig the well. Yes, you're right—it was almost exactly six thousand dollars.

A HUNDRED MILES FROM HEAVEN

As I write about heaven on earth, I wonder, *Why is it that on some days my heart feels like it's a hundred miles from heaven?*

The Bible has a lot to say about the heart, using it as a metaphor of the seat of our soul and our spiritual being. The poet-king David often spoke of his heart for God: "I will praise you, O LORD, with all my heart."[2] And God said of David: "[He is] a man after [my] own heart."[3] My great hope is that one day God will say this of me ... but on some days my heart feels so far away.

If there is a way to a stronger heart for God, what is it? How do I have it?

The way to a strong physical heart is not to rest it. Sitting on the couch watching too many episodes of *Family Guy* will atrophy your heart. Your heart is a giant muscle, and the only way to a ferociously strong heart is to work it out, exhaust it, make it beat hard. Climb a mountain. Do something so difficult your heart feels like it's going to beat right out of your chest.

I believe it works the same spiritually. When you get up and get out and live your life for Christ, your spiritual heart beats stronger. I know this has been true in my life. My most difficult moments have been the moments that have shaped my heart most for God. They are heart-aching, heart-breaking moments I wish I could take back, but I know they have made me more large-hearted and brought me closer to heaven.

I've thought much about what has shaped my heart:

Sitting with a man named Moses when his twin baby daughters died of malaria.

Watching young men play basketball in one shoe, because they only had one shoe apiece.

Giving baths to children whose home is a city dump.

Having to tell a beautiful young woman she is HIV positive.

Seeing women chained together at the ankles on Arizona Avenue.

Watching a close friend in Malawi die of AIDS.

Having people who have less than me share their food and possessions with me.

All I can tell you is what I know: When your heart begins to feel like it's a hundred miles from heaven, give your life away—mentor, serve, give, share, hold, encourage, love … and let God grow your heart.

God grows the hearts of children big. Maybe that's one of the reasons Jesus said, "Come to me like a child."

Sebastian walked into my office a few weeks ago with a great big smile and a giant ziplock bag of change, announcing it was his birthday. "Pastor Palmer, today I'm eight years old, and I'm bringing you one hundred and eight dollars for mosquito nets for kids in Africa."

Our children's ministry had been collecting money to buy mosquito nets for children in Malawi. Sebastian's dad explained to me that his son had been collecting change for months and wanted to make the delivery on his birthday.

It was a great moment. As he handed me the bulging bag of change, he said with resolve, "Next year, on my ninth birthday, I'm bringing you one hundred and nine dollars."

I love it.

Sebastian gave it all. He gave me every last penny to his name—and he didn't have a care in the world. Sebastian didn't have money to put gas in the car to get home, but he wasn't worried. Sebastian didn't have a dime for dinner that night, but it didn't matter to him. He didn't have a cent to his name, literally. But he walked out of my office with a great big Jim Carrey smile on his face. Do you know why? Because he knew his father would take care of it all.

Our heavenly Father has so much more, but we don't live like that. We live more like a two-year-old with a bag of Skittles. You ask him for one, just one, and it's a guaranteed no. You say, "Could I have one? I only want one!" He doesn't care; you're not getting any. Why?

Because for all he knows, this is the last bag of Skittles in the world. You feel like saying to the kid, "Don't you know I have enough money in my wallet to buy you bags and bags of Skittles, enough Skittles to make your stomach ache? If you would just give me *one*."

Live generously,
    love the marginalized,
        free the oppressed,
            show mercy to the hurting,
                give to the poor,
                    and take good news to the lost.

Jesus asks that ordinary, everyday people like you and me become His hands and feet.

So go.
Give your life away.
Take a piece of heaven
to places of hell on earth.

Ideas for Becoming the Expatriate

Teach ESL (English as a Second Language) abroad.
The demand for ESL teachers is especially high in Asian
countries like China and Japan (see www.ELIC.org).

LAYOVER

STUCK IN CUSTOMS

If you've traveled much, then you know there's always a good chance you'll end up getting stuck somewhere … like in customs.

This week my two nephews at Covenant College were heading home on Ethiopian Air to Malawi for Christmas. Side note: I fly a lot of African airlines, but there are a few—and I won't mention names—that I avoid regardless of how cheap they sell their seats! Anyway, as they landed in Addis Ababa a few minutes late, where they were to change planes, they watched their connecting flight pass them on takeoff. They spent the next two days stuck in the Addis Ababa airport.

Yesterday about two thousand train passengers were stuck in the Channel Tunnel that connects London with Paris. The Eurostar train broke down somewhere underneath the English Channel, where the tunnel stretches twenty-three miles! Some walked out. Some just sat there, stuck for more than fifteen hours!

All of us hate being stuck. But sometimes we get stuck in the routine of our own lives, like a Zhu Zhu hamster on a wheel. And when that happens, dreams die.

Churches, too, can get stuck in customs. They do the same thing over and over … and over and over. It all becomes so stale and dry. And people stop growing.

So right now if you're stuck anywhere—in a snowstorm, in immigration, in the DMV, in a life that needs a new dream or a church that needs a new vision … then read this chapter.

This chapter is for everyone stuck in customs.

———◆———

Paul said it to the early church like this,

> *"Everyone who calls on the name of the Lord will be saved." How, then, can they call on the one they have not believed in? And how can they believe in the one of whom they have not heard? And how can they hear without someone preaching to them? And how can they preach unless they are sent?*[1]

The church today must rediscover its *sentness.*[2]

———◆———

This was the second church in a day that a friend and I had visited. Both had recently completed large building projects that rumbled past the fifty-million-dollar mark. As we were guided through the mall-like facility, our guide showed us the shiny new pipes of the million-plus-dollar organ. Impressive. From there we moved to a second surprisingly large auditorium, even for this facility. The room seated more than two hundred, and the ceiling vaulted somewhere around thirty feet into the air. And then we heard, "And in here is our second pipe organ." It, too, cost more than a million dollars!

I felt like I'd entered the Twilight Zone. Two pipe organs in one church?! Why? And I won't say, *Who needs even one?* But don't judge too quickly, because this church also gives hundreds of thousands of dollars to missions every year.

And maybe that says it right there: Having a missions department does not make a church missional.

TINY BUBBLES

Wheaton College students often talk about their hidden but gnawing desire to escape what they refer to as the "Wheaton bubble." In this Thomas Kinkade village, where video arcades are banned along with bars and nightclubs, the tranquil serenity of living in a Christian Mecca can become stifling.

Sometimes the church becomes a *bubble*.

If the church (Christians everywhere) of the twenty-first century has any aspiration of presenting a transformational gospel, then it will need to begin to live out its *sentness*. We all need to take a step back and begin to think differently about our faith—who we are and what is required of us.

The word used today to describe this uprising is *missional.* A movement has begun that is challenging Christians and their churches to look outward, to recapture the passion of the Christ to *go* and make the name of God famous.

The church of tomorrow must embrace its *goingness.* Today the world is flat, but in many ways the church has remained in a bubble.

We can change that.

THE MEDIUM IS THE MESSAGE

I had lunch with Shane Hipps last week. We talked about the architectural design of church buildings and worship auditoriums. He reminded me that *the medium is the message.*[3]

If a church builds a Taj Mahal of a building, then regardless of what they say verbally about the church's values, their message is that the church *building* matters most. This street corner is the end ... rather than a means to an end.

We can easily forget that the local church is meant primarily to be a place where Christ-followers come to encourage and equip one another to go and love as Christ loved. It's a greenhouse for growing trees that will be planted everywhere to flourish and reproduce.

The local church is not the end; it's only the beginning.

If your primary focus is feeding your own church machine, then you will struggle to be missional.

A WORKING DEFINITION

Let me explain what I mean when I use the term *missional.*

Many churches and leaders are latching on to the term without really understanding what the movement is all about. Some have even hijacked the term, using it to describe their church when they have no real missional impetus at all.

At the heart of the missional movement is the idea of the *Missio Dei*—the Mission of God. Michael Frost and Alan Hirsch, pioneers in the missional movement, describe it like this: "The missional church is a sent church. It is a going church; a movement of God through His people; sent to bring healing to a broken world."[4]

I want to briefly explore several ideals that stand out as defining features of the missional church.

COUNTERCULTURAL

The missional church is a countercultural movement. For centuries the Western church has been about the task of getting people to *come* into its churches. Churches hold outreach events to entice people to come to church. Kids get stars on a board when they bring a friend. We sing songs like "Bringing in the Sheaves." Churches invite celebrities and professional athletes to speak and call it *bring your friend Sunday.* None of this is bad or even wrong, but it all gives the subtle message that salvation, hope, and love are only found within the confines of the church.

The church has become like a mission, an outpost in an uncivil, ungodly world. And if lost people can find their way through the front gates, they will be saved. Even the language we use to talk about where we have church, *sanctuary*, implies this is the place of refuge from a clamorous world. Of course the church *is* a place of refuge, and that is good.

But the missional church is first and foremost about sending people out, not just about bringing people in. If a church aspires to be missional, then it will focus the bulk of its energy and resources on sending people *out*.

The missional church does not exist to serve itself; it exists to serve the world. As writer Brett McCraken has said, "Missional is about bringing the church and mission back together. Missions isn't just one of many programs or purpose of church. It is the core, over-arching motivating logic for all we do."[5]

INCLUSIVE

When I was in college, I couldn't afford a Members Only jacket, the microfiber hit of the early eighties, so I settled for a knockoff brand I picked up at Marshall's. I *almost* felt like a member.

This question shouldn't bother me so much, but it does: "So how many members do you have at your church?" It's just that it sounds so elitist. In what way does it matter whether people at our church are members or not? What matters most is that they are participants in a movement. Are people more valuable to the kingdom of Christ if they are members? Or does it matter most to Christ and His kingdom that people love God and others with all their hearts?

There's something about the whole idea of church membership that feels ill-fitting. Maybe we need to think about using different language to express our commitment to the body. I sometimes let this slip out in public, and people audibly gasp. Heresy? I don't think so.

Let's be honest—*membership* is club language. We become members of country clubs and yachting clubs and golf clubs and the Sierra Club. People become members of political parties and fraternities and sororities and Rotary and Lions ... and the list goes on. And if we take an honest look into our souls, we become members so that we can be *in*—which means others are left *out*. I just don't see how this best describes commitment to the church as Christ intended.

The woman named Mary who sinned a lot was let *in*. The short guy who led a tax-extortion ring was let *in*. The water lady with a messed-up marriage history was let *in*. It seems that just about anyone who wanted *in*, Jesus welcomed with open arms.

The Christ said it best like this: "Open the doors. Welcome in anyone and everyone off the street. They're all wanted. This place is for the hurting, the dirty, the dejected, the wanderer, the messed up, the lost, the confused, the broken, the scared, and the scarred."[6] That's the church Christ wanted.

Missional churches will focus less on who is (or is not) allowed in and focus more on who is going out.

At times I feel like the purpose of the church has gone sideways. The church has become a *place* rather than a *people*. We are immobile rather than mobile. Darrel Guder expresses it this way: "Popular grammar captures it well: You 'go to church,' much as the way you go to a store. You 'attend' a church, the way you attend a school or theater. You 'belong to church,' much as you would a service club with its programs and activities."[7]

SIMPLE

I went to college in the eighties with the yuppie, Beemer-driving, Members Only-wearing, mega-consumer generation. The emerging generation is refreshingly simple. And when it comes to church, they still want simple. They are not very interested in performance, dogmatism, personalities, judgmental attitudes, opulence, or mega-anything.

And here's why it makes sense. Following Jesus was simple. Sleep in what you wear. Eat whatever people set in front of you. Live on the go. He said: "Are you ready to rough it? We're not staying in the best inns, you know."[8] Somewhere along the line, we made following Jesus very complicated.

Missional churches value simplicity. For example, their facilities tend to be simple (and to accomplish this I don't mean that churches have to look cheap and junky. There is a significant difference between excellence and opulence). Missional churches create a culture of austerity.

Missional churches also make their programming simple. Years ago I told my staff we would stop trying to match every ministry that churches around us had going. I've visited churches whose list of ministries numbered in the dozens. Bravo, but exhausting. When you run countless ministries to meet every idiosyncratic need of your people, you are practically guaranteed to lose sight of what matters most. When a church boasts countless ministries, you have to wonder—does anyone really know (or care) what the church is most about?

The leadership structure of the missional church is also simple. Churches that love bureaucracy will struggle to be missional. Churches layered with committees and department heads and subcommittees and votes and meetings and more meetings become bogged down in their own political machine and lose their ability to respond and react. They lose their ability to inspire, and they lose their mission—to go. Instead they stay, they become lethargic, they grow big, and ultimately, they become immobile.

One of my first positions in the pastorate was at a church that had mastered the art of church bureaucracy. Without exaggeration, here is the labyrinthine process I was to follow to receive permission for new initiatives: First, I was to take my requests to a Junior High Ministry Advisory Committee, who then reported to the larger Youth Ministry Committee, which fell under the authority of the Christian Education Committee, which was under the jurisdiction of the Administrative Council, who then took my request to the Board of Elders. It took months to get approval to replenish my supply of water balloons (okay, not really, not the water balloon part).

The missional church, on the other hand, chooses decision-making processes that are efficient. Its aim is to mobilize as economically and expediently as possible.

HYPEROPTIC

Hyperopia is the opposite of myopia, or nearsightedness. The missional church's focus is hyperoptic—it looks out. It is more farsighted than nearsighted. The missional church refuses to become enveloped by its own wants and needs. Like a beautiful but antiquated 1977 Cadillac Eldorado, the church can become a beast of a machine that takes every ounce of creative energy and available resources just to keep running.

If you think about it, much of what happens in churches is focused inward. Dan Kimball writes, "The average church focuses most efforts on the quality of the programs and ministries to keep those already attending happy, rather than on our biblical mission."[9] The programs are for people already there. The language used is only understood by those on the inside: blood, sacrifice, ministry, tithe, atonement, fellowship, regeneration, bless, and the list goes on.

By necessity, a vast percentage of most churches' resources is spent on keeping the machine running. Programs cost money. Advertising costs money. AC, carpet cleaning, landscaping, Krispy Kreme doughnuts, and I-MAG units cost money. It's easy to give into these demands and allow the immediate to dictate the important.

A church in Simi Valley, California, had outgrown its worship auditorium, so they talked about buildings and capital campaigns and expanding their campus. Finally, after hearing the monumental amount of the final budget, the pastor said, "Forget it. We'll meet outside. We'll take the money we were going to raise for a new building and put it into missions and give it away." And they did, and they are.

Not every church sits in the utopian, year-round perfect climate of Simi Valley, but you get my point. If we spend less on the machine in here, we can give more to people out there.

MAKE JESUS FAMOUS

The missional church is first and foremost committed to making the name of Jesus Christ famous. There's a simple but profound return to Jesus—just Jesus. The message is about Jesus. Pastors and personalities are not what matter most. Church buildings and programs are not why the church exists. Jesus Christ is the roaring center of everything missional.

Beginning with the idea of the incarnation, the missional church models its function after the life and ministry of Christ. In the New Testament, Jesus' close friend John said it like this, "[He] made his dwelling among us."[10] Jesus poured Himself into the world He lived in and into the lives of those He lived among—this is the incarnation. In the same way, the church today must give all it's worth to the world out there—locally and globally.

GRASSROOTS

A distinct feature of being missional is that it is more a movement than an institution. Historically the church has depended heavily on the institutional structure of denominations. Yet today's emerging generation of Christ-followers often seeks to be free of this kind of structure. Alan Roxburgh observes, "Once-proud mainline denominations are bleeding members every year."[11]

American denominationalism emerged in the nineteenth century as a form of tribalism. As immigrants flooded the eastern seaboard from Europe, they sought to identify with people groups from their homelands. So the Germans formed the Lutheran tribe. The Scots, with their Reformed roots, formed the Presbyterian tribe. The Swedes who found comfort in the Minnesota tundra formed the Evangelical Free tribe. And the list goes on. Denominations give you a place to belong while at the same time, whether intentionally or unintentionally, their ideological boundaries provide a means to keep others out.

I find it amusing when I meet individuals who tell me about the "nondenominational" church they attend. I'll sometimes say, "Now, you do know they are part of a denomination, right?"

"No, they're not; we've been there for years, and no one has ever mentioned a denomination," they protest.

And that's my point. It's not that these churches disagree with or are ashamed of their denomination, but they rightfully desire to communicate to their world that *the doors are open*. And that is good.

UNCOMFORTABLE

Between bites of Nello's Pizza, Shane Hipps went on to talk about speaking at Rob Bell's church, Mars Hill. When he stood in the middle of the large auditorium, the first thing he said was, "Whether you know it or not, the chairs you sit on are part of your message at Mars Hill." Everyone literally squirmed to take a peek at the chair under them—molded grey plastic. "The chairs are inexpensive, hard, and rather uncomfortable. The chairs are quietly saying to you, 'Don't get too comfortable, don't stay too long. Your place in this world is out there, not in here.'"

So look outward more and inward less. Begin to think differently about church. Church is not most about buildings or programs or personalities. You are the church, and God wants you to go. It's time to rediscover our *sentness*.

The medium is the message.

Ideas for Becoming the Expatriate

Drive the neighborhoods around your church until you find the home that needs the most TLC. Then (with the owner's permission) come back on Saturday with your friends to mow, weed, trim the yard, and paint the entire house.

CHAPTER 6

DO LOVE

The Bible has a lot to say about feet—seriously. Where our feet lead us, how they need washing, and then, surprisingly, how beautiful they are.

Paul, who walked all over the Middle East, wrote these words: "As it is written, 'How beautiful are the feet of those who bring good news!'"[1]

Jesus showed that it was good to wash the feet of others as an act of love. If you love people, you care about their feet.

Jesus was having dinner at His friend Simon's home when a woman embroiled in sin stopped in. Anytime someone like that shows up for dinner, there's going to be a scene. Simon's friends tried to run her off. Simon questioned her motives. But Jesus objected: "Let her wash feet. Let her show her love. Her many sins are forgiven. She is loving much."[2]

If your life is full of sin and you discover the wideness of God's mercy, then love much. Give more love away.

LOVE MUCH

Every time I walked through the café doors of the rustic Santiago de Cuba hotel, Bobby's four-piece band would break into the sultry Brazilian ballad "Girl from Ipanema." The band knew by now that I would respond with loud applause and a generous tip on my way out, guaranteeing I would again be greeted by my favorite Latin tune when I returned.

Over the course of our stay in this quiet oceanside hotel, the basketball players and I became well acquainted with Bobby and his band. As we left to speak in churches around the city each evening, my guys would always invite the band. Each night they politely had an excuse. I was not surprised. They were all generous day drinkers and spent their free time flirting with the friendly prostitutes who lingered outside the hotel. But on our final night in Santiago, the entire band showed up at the church we were visiting. The church was overcrowded, and the band appeared uncomfortable and out of place, but it was a great gesture on their part.

At the time I did not sense much of a response. The following day we checked out of the hotel. As we were leaving, one of our players, Dan Linsz, gave Bobby a Bible and his basketball shoes. As we walked across the steamy tarmac toward our Cubana Air jet, Dan told me about his gift to Bobby. My honest thoughts were, *I'm sure Bobby is excited about the shoes, but I really can't picture him ever reading the Bible.* And as we walked up the steel staircase to our plane, I doubted we would ever see Bobby again.

Two years later Dan returned to Santiago with me when I took a band, Kepano Green, to Cuba. While in Santiago, we returned to Second Baptist Church, the same church our players spoke in on our final night in Cuba two years earlier. The church was packed, dozens of people even crowded outside each window trying to get a glimpse of the American band. After the concert and my message, I looked up to see Bobby making his way to the front, beaming.

I was greeted with a smothering Cuban hug, and before we could untangle, he blurted out, "I'm a Christian now!" And next to him were his two daughters and his wife.

The pastor of Second Baptist, Elmer Lavastida, came over to say, "Yes, Bobby is one our most faithful Christians now; his life has turned upside down."

Bobby went on to share his story. "Palmer, I was a drunk (no surprise there), and I was a terrible father and husband. I cheated on my wife, and I was not a good person. But your basketball team changed me. No one has ever given me such a gift as the shoes from Dan. When I began wearing the shoes I started thinking about the Bible. And I began to read it. The more I read the more convicted I became that my life needed to change. So I returned to the church where your team spoke and met Pastor Lavastida. He helped me to accept Jesus Christ as my Savior. Since then my life has completely changed. And just last week my wife and daughters were baptized with me."

Dan and I were both floored to realize that the simple gift of shoes and a Bible could so radically transform a life. Beautiful.

I'm not sharing this to say something really trite like, "Give your shoes away, and people will become Christians." What I am trying to say is "Love much." God uses you to change lives when you love much.

———————

We don't think a whole lot about shoes in America. We take shoes for granted. You can buy a rather sturdy pair of nameless shoes for practically nothing. Our most expensive shoes are worn on the asphalt basketball courts of inner cities. We never wear shoes until they wear out. Our closets are cluttered with dated shoes we simply tired of wearing or think have gone out of something called "style."

In the developing world, however, shoes arouse a mysterious passion. A decent pair of leather shoes is usually far too expensive for most people. Grown men and woman spend entire days laboring in fields or factories to afford a pair of thin plastic flip-flops, something we would only consider wearing to the beach or to check our mail. The dress shoes sold in the markets are made of cheap vinyl that heats up under the tropical sun. A good pair of shoes is a prized possession.

In Malawi, practically any shoe is a luxury. Lilongwe, the capital, is maybe the only African city where I have seen grown men walking the streets downtown barefoot. They are ashamed, I know that, but they have no choice. So I was not surprised when I took our college basketball team from Wheaton to our first practice in the African Bible College gym and two of the Malawians in the gym were scrimmaging with only one shoe on.

Several of our players began to snicker and point out to one another how funny it was that two guys were playing with a shoe on one foot and the other foot bare. One of them turned to my twin brother, who had lived in Malawi for more that ten years and was coaching the Malawian National Team, and asked why these guys were playing ball in just one shoe.

His answer was sobering: "One of the guys showed up today with no shoes. His friend did not want him to be ashamed when you arrived, so he lent him one of his own. Now they both have at least one shoe."

The laughter stopped.

But here is what's great. After seeing the need in Malawi, Graham, one of the basketball players from Wheaton, returned to college and began a scholarship program to send Malawians to college, completely funded by him and the guys in his dorm! Now realize this—guys at Wheaton College are perpetually broke. When they run out of food on the weekends, they go dumpster diving, which means they drive around to local grocery stores and dig through their dumpsters looking for discarded cans of food or day-old bread and produce. These were college students pooling their limited resources to send fellow college students in Africa to school. Beautiful.

HOW LOVE WORKS

Love as God loves. His love is deep and lasting and intimate. He loves you on the sunny days, and He loves you on the rainy days. He loves you in the morning, and He loves you at night. He loves you on the days you wander and on the days you wonder if anyone cares.

But if you are one who lives in the love of God, then know this—you are His hands from heaven. Yes, *you*. You are the means by which the love of God is scattered all over this world. You are His hands and His feet.

My wife has a bias against feet. She says feet are gross and gets bugged when my feet touch her in bed. Yet she's constantly begging me to massage her aching feet, especially after she's put in a long day teaching junior highers. We all end up with days when our feet ache—but who ever really cares? Maybe God does.

The psalmists often wrote about the ways God cares for feet. They write that He won't let them slip, He keeps them from stumbling on rocks, and He guides them in dark places.[3]

When you truly love people, you care about their pain—yes, even their aching feet. So if you intend to spread the love God has shown you, then do it. You are His hands. And feet.

One sticky Saturday afternoon in the Liberian jungle when I was nine, my father had our family walking for hours—again—to reach a remote village where he was to preach. About four hours into our bush trek, we suddenly burst into a small clearing with a quaint American-style home, manicured lawn, flowering plants and bushes, and two white people sitting on their front porch, sipping cold drinks. The entire scene was a bit surreal.

Of course we stopped. I didn't know there were white people within a hundred miles of our jungle trail. My parents greeted them and began what seemed to be a strained conversation. I anxiously waited for the white people to invite us in out of the tropical heat for some ice-cold lemonade or maybe even a Coke!

My feet ached, and my body was soaked with sweat from the stinkin' polyester shirt my mom had made me wear that day. I waited for the invitation to come in and sit down—my feet really hurt—and waited—I was so thirsty—and waited.

The couple never asked us in.

We started to walk again, back into the jungle, leaving the pleasant white people behind us. It all felt rather odd.

I later asked my father why the white people never invited us into their home to sit down and have a cold drink. It really bothered me because we lived in the jungle too, and we never let strangers leave without treating them as honored guests.

"They didn't ask us in," my dad explained, "because they are Christians who are only friends with Christians from their church."

We weren't from their kind of church. Not so beautiful.

Please don't try to tell people about God without first giving His love away.

Jesus fumed, "I was thirsty and you gave me nothing to drink."[4]

When I was nine, my feet hurt, and you gave me nowhere to sit down.

Do love.

———

As we stood outside our home watching it burn, I knew absolutely everything we owned was inside. I was eight years old. Just two years earlier, my family had moved into the Sappo rainforest in Liberia, some of world's most dense jungle. The only way into our remote mission station was to fly in on a single-engine Cessna 180. The local Christians had built us a grand bamboo-mat house. And as far as bamboo-mat houses go, this one was sweet. It sat three feet off the ground on stilts, had a wood floor and a new tin roof. The porch was screened in, and for some reason, the entire perimeter of the house had a one-foot-wide ledge at floor level outside. We would wake up every morning to the sound of goats jockeying for space on the ledge and to the sight of about a dozen village kids standing on the ledge with their faces pressed against the screen, peering in on the life of the *nyomplu* (that's what the village kids called my twin brother and me in the local Sapo language—it means white spirit—and yes, rather unnerving when you're eight).

My family enjoyed the bamboo-mat house for two years, but one afternoon, the mat house next to ours caught fire. It went up like a gasoline-soaked torch, and the flames leapt over to our home. It burned quickly. When we ran out, we had little time to take anything with us. My dad, in a state of confusion, ran into the burning house. Ignoring cash, jewelry, equipment, passports, and furniture, he emerged with his arms loaded with jars of wild-berry jam my mom had just made. He loved the stuff.

Everything we owned, everything American, burned. As we stood on the grass airfield watching our home burn to the ground, I turned and looked at my fifteen-year-old sister, Lisa, who stood beside me sobbing, barefoot. She didn't even make it out with her shoes. As she wept, a young Liberian girl, one of Lisa's friends, stepped up next to her and held her in an embrace, then took the shoes off her feet and slipped them on Lisa's feet. Beautiful.

People ask why a good friend of mine, Coach John Lott, and I loaded six-hundred-plus pairs of shoes into a shipping container earlier this year to send to Liberia, a country impoverished and recovering from fifteen years of civil war. Maybe this is why. Maybe it's because the Liberians loved much when my family had little, so I, too, want to love much in return.

Coach Lott is the Cardinals' strength and conditioning coach and runs his annual Get-Your-Mind-Right football camp at The Grove. Every kid who signs up for the camp is required to bring a pair of shoes for kids in Liberia. John also brings in shoes by the bag-full from Cardinal players. Anquan Boldin, Kurt Warner, Larry Fitzgerald, and about a dozen other players all send their extra shoes over to go in the shipping container headed to Africa. It doesn't take much to share much.

I left Liberia when Charles Taylor's rebel forces were wreaking havoc on the country. Not long after I left, one of my college students, Summerville Bryant, was walking through the streets of his coastal hometown of Buchanan. He hadn't been home long, and his family was glad to have him back as war broke out across the country. So as he walked through town with his younger brother, they held hands, as African men often do as a sign of deep friendship.

A rebel boy-soldier stopped them when he spotted Summerville's brother's basketball high-tops. "Give me your shoes!" he demanded.

The shoes were nice, real American-made basketball shoes. Naturally, the thirteen-year-old boy hesitated in protest. Without asking a second time, the child-soldier raised his M16 and in one motion, shot him in the chest. Summerville was still holding his brother's hand as he slumped to the ground, dead. While Summerville screamed in agony, the rebel pulled the shoes off the brother's feet, slipped them on his own, and walked away.

If people are dying over something as simple as shoes, then shouldn't we do more to share what we have with those who don't?

I think we all need the passion of IUPUI (Indiana University-Purdue University Indianapolis) basketball coach Ron Hunter. On his recruiting trips to Africa, Coach Hunter became bothered by the sight of so many barefoot people. In response, Hunter invited students and the community to donate shoes. To promote the cause, he promised to coach an entire NCAA game barefoot.

He did, against Oakland University. Coach Hunter's goal was to send 40,000 pairs of shoes to Nigeria. By tip-off he already had 110,000 pairs! And they won the game.

LOVE FIRST

Physical needs are real needs. Never miss that. Jesus was always concerned with how people were doing physically. We often mistakenly view Jesus as a traveling Bible-belt evangelist who went from town to town to preach, give an invitation, then bolt. Not so; He stopped to love.

Jesus always loved first. Before He told the adulterous woman to "sin no more," He stopped her accusers from attacking. Before Jesus told the blind man He was the Christ, He gave him sight. Before He told the man from Bethesda to stop sinning, He told him to get up and walk. Before He told the infected man to thank God, He cured him of leprosy. Jesus always met the physical needs of hurting people first.

Don't mistake this for evangelical manipulation. Jesus did not heal with the aim of, "If I heal them, maybe this will cause them to want God." We see no such pattern. Jesus met the needs of hurting people for one reason—LOVE. He loved first. He loved much.

SIMPLY LIVE

My brother Del, who's lived all over Africa, loves this quote: "Live simply so that others may simply live."[5]

Western culture is everything but simple. We are a complicated people, and we like our stuff. Will Samson writes about American stuff; he says that in 1901, 21 percent of what we owned was nonessential. Today, more than 50 percent of what we own is nonessential![6]

In the Bible, Solomon said, "God made us plain and simple, but we have made ourselves very complicated."[7] He was speaking from experience. He had a lot of stuff.

Nobel Prize-winner and world-renowned scholar Albert Schweitzer spent much of his career traveling on trains. Someone once asked him why he always traveled third class, and his answer was plain and simple: "There [is] no fourth class."[8]

Philip Yancey reflected on a trip he made to a monastery. After the monk showed him his small room, he said, "If you need anything, let us know and we'll teach you how to get along without it."[9]

What makes us think we must have so much and are entitled to have the newest and the best?

Jesus once came across a young man who wanted to follow Him. The man asked what must be done. Jesus knew he was wealthy and owned a lot, so He hit him where it hurts. He said, "You still lack one thing—give it all away ... then come and follow Me."[10]

Jesus was saying, "You don't need so much stuff. You don't need so many houses and barns and cows and sheep and tents and fifty-two-inch plasma screens."

I sometimes wonder, how much is enough? How many cars? How much money? How many golf clubs? How many square feet? How much jewelry? How many outfits? How many pairs of shoes does one person need?

BAREFOOT SUNDAY

We dubbed this past Sunday at The Grove "Barefoot Sunday." It was the final day of our Serve the World Week, and I was hoping people would get the idea that each one of us can make a difference in a hurting world. I asked everyone to come to church wearing their best and favorite shoes, then to take them off and go home barefoot. Our team heading to Africa would pack the shoes and give them away.

I've never heard of a church anywhere trying something this whacked, but I really did believe that leaving church barefoot would help our people get the idea. If you are convinced this world is a broken place, and if you fully believe your life—your one and most important life—can make a difference, then you will care less about things like shoes and more about loving people who hurt.

When I first shared my idea over dinner, my son in elementary school said, "Don't do it, Dad. People will stay home!" His brother in high school agreed.

When I told my staff, the first response I got was, "Won't people be breaking the law when they drive home barefoot?" Such an American reaction. Another staff member suggested we pass out Japanese slippers so people's feet wouldn't burn on the hot asphalt.

What?

It was September; it can't get that hot in September … even in Arizona.

I had a guy at church build three crates to put on stage to hold the shoes. Another staff member said, "Oh no, he built them too big. We'll never fill them."

My wife looked at the forecast on Saturday and said, "Uh-oh,

Palmer, it's going to be a record high of one hundred and seven degrees tomorrow—people really will burn their feet."

"Sweet," I responded. "They'll remember what it feels like to go barefoot."

But I could hardly sleep that night.... All night I kept thinking about people staying home, barefoot-driving citations, empty crates, and blistering feet. I had refused to buy the Japanese slippers.

I got to church early, around six, and found an overnight parcel sitting by my office door. Inside was a pair of shoes from my friend Don in Colorado Springs. He said he didn't want to miss out on Barefoot Sunday. I felt it was going to be a very good day.

We had record high attendance that day—in all three services. People didn't stay home. What I didn't anticipate was, not only did people leave the shoes they wore, many brought bags of shoes with them. By the time the morning was over, we had mountains of shoes spilling over and around all three crates; somewhere around two thousand pairs of shoes!

I had two sisters come up to me after the third service. One said, "Palmer, when I got home after the nine-thirty service I felt convicted that we had too many shoes in the house. So I filled two bags with every pair we owned. Then I went to my sister's house and told her she needed to do the same thing."

"And I've never even been to The Grove," her sister piped up with a smile.

They bagged up every shoe in the sister's house and brought them all back to The Grove.

Then they said, "But pray for us, Palmer; our husbands weren't home when we took all the shoes, and we think they may be a bit surprised when they get back."

You think?

I met a couple who came to The Grove for the very first time on Barefoot Sunday. I thought, *Oh no, they're going to think this is way weird.* They chose to go home barefoot.

Giving away a pair of shoes doesn't solve world poverty, I know that, but it does remind me to live simply. It does remind me, "I can live with less!"

It was a blazing one hundred and seven degrees on Barefoot Sunday; plus, we had just resealed the parking lot bright black, so it sizzled like a frying pan.

It was perfect.

But my point wasn't just to have a shoe drive. I wanted everyone, in a small way, to experience what 1.3 billion people feel every day. Going barefoot hurts.

I challenged people to spend the rest of the day barefoot. One entire family went shopping at a department store barefoot. For all who went out to lunch that day, the phrase "No shirt, no shoes, no service" took on a whole new meaning. At Pei Wei, I kept looking over my shoulder, hoping the manager wouldn't notice my bare feet and kick me out. Going barefoot is humiliating.

But you and I can change that, even if it's just one pair of feet at a time.

ALL THINGS GO

In our country, people spend six billion dollars a year in beauty salons getting manicures and pedicures; that's billion with a *b*. I think we forget the world is broken.

I know guys who get pedicures. I tell them a man shouldn't do that—plus, it costs a ridiculous amount to have someone scrub and sand your toes. Don't do it. Gnaw on them if you have to.

Could you picture Chuck Liddell getting a pedicure? I doubt it. How about Chuck Norris? Never. Would Dog the Bounty Hunter? Not a chance.

I'm not trying to get you to give more money. I simply want to challenge you to live differently. Live to love much. And that may mean not wasting time and money on pedicures.

Care more about the feet of others. That's how Jesus lived.

I don't intend to be harsh, but let's stop being so obsessed with our own pleasure and possessions and start giving our lives away.

All things go.

No *thing* lasts forever.

But people do.

Ideas for Becoming the Expatriate

Initiate a Barefoot Sunday at your church, or hold a Barefoot Day at your college or work place. Invite everyone to come in their best and favorite pair of shoes ... and go home barefoot. Then give the shoes away in places like Sierra Leone, Haiti, or Bangladesh. (see www.BarefootSunday.org)

PART IV

DESIRE

Love the Lord your God with all your heart.

I traveled about as deep as you can go into Côte d'Ivoire interior to the festering town of Danané, near the Liberian border. The Liberian civil war had been raging for a year, and thousands of Liberians had fled across the border and ended up in grimy places like Danané.

I came looking for college students I knew. Many had fled there from Liberia, and I wanted to encourage them and share with them as much as I could bring. I showed up with five suitcases stuffed with shirts and shoes … and basketballs. Hey, even refugees want to hoop it up—and we did.

The African Bible College students came from all over. Dozens of them. I wished I had more suitcases.

One of my students, Sam Weah, who was still living in Liberia, made the fifty-mile trip, much of it on foot, to come see me. When he walked through the door, I greeted him with a big hug … and he grimaced. I let go. "I'm sorry—what's wrong, Sam?"

"It's the wounds on my back. I'll show you." Taking off his shirt, he turned to show me dozens of gaping wounds. Sam went on to tell me the story of his stripes.

A couple of weeks earlier, he had been returning to Liberia from Côte d'Ivoire with money for his ministry and church members. The young rebel soldiers who controlled the border knew he was returning with money, so to have an excuse for robbing him, they charged him with spying for the Liberian government. They stripped him to his underwear and for three days whipped him with a fan belt. When they finally released him, his back was slashed raw.

The third day after Sam's release was a Wednesday. He gingerly got out of bed and started to dress himself.

"What are you doing?" his wife questioned.

"It's Wednesday. You know on Wednesdays I teach the Bible study at the border for the rebel soldiers."

"Sure, I know that, Sam. But they just beat you raw for three days. You can't go back there," she pleaded.

"I must."

He picked up his Bible and limped the three miles back to where he had been imprisoned and interrogated.

When the rebel soldiers saw him coming, they began to shout at him, "What are you doing here, Pastor? We already released you."

"Don't you know today is Wednesday? You know that every Wednesday we have prayer and Bible study. So call the boys. I'm here to pray with you."

As usual, they started with singing. Sam said they sang louder than ever before. Then Sam asked one of the rebel soldiers to read the Bible passage for the day—the man who just days before had beat him mercilessly with the fan belt.

That afternoon, a dozen rebels prayed with Sam to receive Jesus Christ as their Lord and Savior.

Some people will go regardless of the cost.

CHAPTER 7

OVERLANDER

The Brussels Air jumbo jet raced down the Abidjan runway at full throttle. I had just spent two weeks in Africa with two teams of people giving their lives away—one team in Malawi and the other in the steamy Liberian jungle. It felt good to have the plane's AC blowing on me full blast. After a week of drinking river water poured through a sand filter, I was looking forward to a cold drink that I could trust. I had been told the thing purified the water, but my stomach told me something different.

So as the Airbus 330 raced down the runway, I relaxed prematurely. I leaned my seat back, loosened my seat belt, and kicked off my shoes.... Never do that! No sooner had I closed my eyes when BOOM—there was a loud explosion off to the right side of the aircraft.

DESIRE

As I mentioned earlier, when you get on an airplane and look down, your perspective always changes. In much the same way, when you go and give your life away, your desires and passions change.

In the Shema, the Jewish people recite the powerful line, "Love the LORD your God with all your heart."[1]

Jesus stressed the importance of having a right heart for this world: "You're blessed when you get your inside world—your mind and heart—put right. Then you can see God in the outside world."[2]

The Bible has much to say about giving your heart to God. The transformed life is evidenced by a new and powerful desire for God. God grips the heart. When He has our lives, we have new allegiances and passions. God spoke through His prophet Ezekiel and said, "I'll give you a new heart, put a new spirit in you. I'll remove the stone heart from your body and replace it with a heart that's God-willed, not self-willed."[3] The writers of the Bible used the metaphor of the heart as the seat of right or wrong desires. When people noticed their need for new desires, we read, "They were cut to the heart."[4]

I've boiled life down to two ways you can live. One, you can live optimistically and full of passion; or, two, you can live pessimistically and full of apathy. I'm convinced that if God has your heart, you will live with a passionate desire to give Him, this world, this life everything you've got.

And here's what I invite you to wrestle with right now: Do you know, without a shadow of a doubt, what God wants with your life? What is it that God wants to accomplish through you and in you during your short time in this world?

DESIRE HEART CHANGE

Transformation is what makes Christian education unique from other forms of education, because the end goal of all Christian pedagogy is *heart change,* or as the Bible says, "a new heart." Knowing God brings a new way of living.

Formal education is primarily concerned with intellectual change, as opposed to life change. The assumption educators make is that cognitive knowledge is sufficient; if learners *know,* then they will *do* what they know. This is simply a false assumption.

Perry Downs, my adviser at Trinity International University, explains that what is missing is the *will* to do what we know must be done.[5] You and I need this heart-of-God *desire* (will, passion, resolve, determination) to change what is morally wrong.

A direct line does not lead from what we *know* to what we *do.* A heart change must transpire, creating a *desire* to do what we know is good.

When I taught college in Liberia, practically every day women from across the border in Guinea came by our home selling fruit and vegetables. They would walk up our drive, yelling, "Missy, banana, gre-fru, paw-paw, or-ing!" over and over, and rather loudly, until someone came out of the house to buy something. I found the whole thing rather annoying, and when I did go out to remind them that we had just bought piles of oranges and bananas and grapefruit from them the day before, I was usually a bit short.

But then, one sizzling dry-season afternoon, I saw the whole crowed of Guinea women sitting with Bill and Pat Clark, our neighbors, having ice-cold lemonade on their porch. Then I saw them—for the first time, I really looked at their faces. Sweat was running down their foreheads; walking door to door with a load of grapefruit on your head for hours in the noonday African sun is exhausting. For the first time, I noticed their sweet smiles as they chatted with the Clarks. For the first time, I really saw them.

I went home that night and said, "Veronica, we need to start giving the Guinea women drinks when they come by."

"Why?"

"Because the Clarks are," I joked.

The truth is that this godly couple, who gave their lives to loving people in Africa, showed me what I had missed—faces, names, and stories.

We started to give the women something cold to drink, learning their names and practicing a few French phrases.

Here's the thing. I *knew* Jesus' words as well as any Christian: "I was thirsty and you gave me nothing to drink."[6] But *knowing* what He said was not affecting what I *did*. When my heart was affected, my desire to *do* what I knew followed.

We are all a bit like that. What we *know* does not always change what we *do*. Simply teaching moral values is not enough.

The will (or heart, as the Bible refers to the seat of our spiritual passion) must be affected. Teaching moral content is good, but unless we lead people to new moral desires, we fail.

RESISTANCE

The moment you determine to change this world for good, you will have a dozen good reasons not to. It happens to all of us. We think noble thoughts about ending poverty and stopping injustice, but life seems to always get in the way.

In his quirky but insightful short read, *The War of Art*, Steven Pressfield explores the problem of resistance. He asks,

> Are you a born writer? Were you put on earth to be a painter, a scientist, an apostle of peace? In the end the question can only be answered by action. Do it or don't do it.... If ... you don't do it ... [y]ou shame the angels who watch over you and you spite the Almighty, who created you and only you with your unique gifts, for the sole purpose of nudging the human race one millimeter farther along its path back to God.... Don't cheat us of your contribution. Give us what you've got.[7]

We've all been there.

Everyone who has a pulse has experienced resistance, and it usually comes in the form of procrastination. We have a desire to do something new and bold and good ... but for one reason or another never get around to it.

If you've ever bought a treadmill you know all about resistance—because it's sitting in the garage collecting dust. You know resistance if you've ever dreamed about starting your own business, finishing college, doing art, learning to play the guitar, or doing anything noble to change this world for good.

Resistance hits us from all sides. Parents tell us it's a poor life choice. Teachers tell us we can't do it. Friends laugh at our ideas. Professionals in the field tell us we're naive.

Jesus faced this kind of resistance. He opened the eyes of a blind man, but religious people resisted. "It's the Sabbath day," they protested. You see, people will even resist the good we do when the good we do is not so good in their eyes.

As Doc Hendley tended bar in Raleigh and overheard conversations, he was surprised at how much people talked about the world's problems and what needed to be done to fix them. Then it hit him: Even people who go to bars care about helping people who hurt! So he asked the bar owner for permission, at closing time—rather than having a "last call" for drinks—to have a call for donations for wells in Africa. The idea was whacked, but the owner agreed.

Money poured in … no pun intended.

Doc really had no idea what to do with the money. He tried to give it away, but he couldn't find anyone who could guarantee a well would be dug. Plus, a lot of people weren't so sure that accepting money from bars for wells was such a good idea. So Doc left the bar, left Raleigh, and started digging wells—all over Africa. He calls his work Wine to Water.[8]

I'm not saying go drink more so wells can be dug in Africa. But I am saying when you have a life-changing, life-saving idea, don't let other people stop your dreaming.

When God fills you with desire, find resolve.

My friend Zach says children have no fear to dream and create—because they know their parents will only rain down praise. Your Father in heaven is like that.

Practically all of us live in two worlds. One is the commuting-for-two-hours, changing-diapers, visiting-the-in-laws, watching-the-*Dancing-with-the-Stars*-rerun, unloading-the-dishwasher, meeting-with-the-tired-small-group-that-shares-the-same-prayer-requests-every-week world. This world has hijacked our lives.

The other world is the world we dream of living in one day. That world is filled with possibility and passion. It's the world of new ideas and risks and adventure. This is the world we talk about and hope about … but all too often, this is the world we never find. For one reason or another it remains the life unlived.

Overlanders are large four-wheel-drive trucks transformed into open-air buses. The people on them, also called Overlanders, travel across Africa through game parks, stopping to white-water raft, hike, and spend time sightseeing in towns and villages along the way. The experience usually lasts at least a month and can be exhausting—yet at the same time exhilarating.

I've talked to Overlanders who spill out of their trucks in Lilongwe grimy and dust-covered, looking for a cold drink or something to eat. Wherever they camp, they say, the beds are hard, the food is never great, the roads beat you ragged, but the experience of roaming Africa in the back of a truck is something they would trade for nothing else.

———

The most pronounced resistance we encounter is internal. We secretly fear the unknown, so we fail to act on what we know must be done. We make excuses about the time not being right. We say we need just a little more education. We promise that when all the bills are paid, or when the kids are big enough, or when things slow down at work … and the list goes on.

But there are some things we cannot wait to do. The timing may never be just right, the circumstances may never be quite what you want, all the money may never be there … but do it anyway. Because that perfect day might never come.

Pressfield says fear is an indicator of what you must do!

> Resistance is experienced as fear; the degree of
> fear equates the strength of Resistance. Therefore
> the more fear we feel about a specific enterprise,
> there more certain we can be that that enterprise
> is important to us and to the growth of our soul.
> That's why we feel so much Resistance. If it
> meant nothing to us, there'd be no Resistance.[9]

If you feel any degree of fear or anxiety about acting on the desire God has put in your soul—then you must do it.

Live the desires of your heart.

God has put you here to do certain good for Him—you, and only you. Not your parents, not your friends, not your pastors—*you*.

Fight resistance.

Find resolve.

ETERNAL DESIRES

Death has been on my mind lately. Karl Barth says, "We say we believe we will die but we don't really believe it." We live like this life will last forever.

It won't.

I was teaching through the ancient wisdom of Solomon in Ecclesiastes recently and noticed that my Bible titled one section *Death Comes to All*. Wow. Cheery.

I heard of an Internet site called DeathClock.com that will calculate the exact date of your final day on earth. It dubs itself, "The Internet's friendly reminder that life is slipping away." Who needs that? I went there anyway, plugged in a few innocuous pieces of information, and the Death Clock told me that Palmer Chinchen will meet his Maker on Thursday, August 13, 2037. What? That's coming up quickly!

I didn't like that answer at all. Plus, I felt the Clock was short on information; I don't drink, I've cut back on my Krispy Kreme intake … but it didn't ask for any of this important information. Here's the good news. You can cheat death on the Internet. I searched and found another site, called something like The Death Calculator. I liked its answer better: My final day on earth is scheduled for Thursday, January 14, 2051. Then it told me I've lived 51.2 percent of my life. A Lipitor ad blinked at the bottom of the page—"If life is good, why not extend it?"

You can't.

NINETY DAYS

Do you ever wonder how you would live if you were told you had just ninety days left? Would you live any differently? What would you do with those days?

Another Web site, 43things.com, allows you to join others in making a list of things you want to do before dying. Here are a few things people listed: fall in love, get a tattoo, learn to surf, meet the Dalai Lama, pay off my student loans (I would sure hope so!), learn Spanish, change the world, quit my job, move out, backpack through Europe, dance in the rain, make more friends, pray.

The recent movie *The Bucket List* made popular the idea of doing everything you've ever dreamed of doing before you die. But in a very real way, skydiving, bungee jumping, and seeing the Taj Mahal and the Great Wall of China just don't mean that much. Really. There's got to be more.

MOMENTS MATTER

If you have just one life to live, and your life is a most important life, then by all means, make it matter.

If I had just ninety days, every moment would carry meaning. Driving my kids to school would no longer be a chore, but a joy. I would never hurry through dinner with friends. I would stop taking naps. I might live with some urgency, I might not procrastinate, I would not wait for tomorrow. Most importantly, I would give my life to Christ and His kingdom. I would try to stop making this life all about me and make it more about Him. I would do my best to live that way *today*.

If you have just ninety days, then there are no average days. There are no throwaway days. God opens doors and gives opportunities, but He also takes them away. You don't have potential forever. David asked that God not allow him to forget this truth: "LORD, remind me how brief my time on earth will be. Remind me that my days are numbered—how fleeting my life is. You have made my life no longer than the width of my hand. My entire lifetime is just a moment to you; at best, each of us is but a breath."[10]

If you don't value today, you are sure to live with regrets.

Dying while healthy, rich, and free enough to drink life to the last drop gets great press, but I'm not sure everyone knows what to do with their lives, even if they only had ninety days!

PASSION MATTERS

Solomon wrote much about passion: "Whatever your hand finds to do, do it with all your might."[11]

Have passion that matters. You can have passion for something that isn't worth a dime. It's entirely possible to waste passion and energy on things that are meaningless.

Let me tell you how to waste your passion.

I watch people pour themselves into coffee. I'm a fellow addict, but it's just a drink. Really. I was loitering at Starbucks, nursing a grande coffee-of-the-day, when I couldn't help but overhear the commotion being made by a woman unhappy with her concoction. She had ordered some ridiculous mix that would take a chemist to get right—something like a half-caf-sugar-free-venti-soy-double-shot-triple-hot-mocha-latte. She was returning it for the third time; I'm not exaggerating. This lady was making a scene, telling the barista how incompetent she was. I wanted to tell her to zip it. Who cares? It's just a coffee. Really.

Have passion for something that matters. Change a life. Pour yourself into people.

GIVE IT YOUR ALL

I had been helping one of my sons with his homework; he was supposed to write a few things about Magellan. For the very first time, I learned how this world explorer died: He was chased by angry natives on a beach in the Philippines and killed by spears and arrows. So here's my thought—dying's not good, but if you are a world-renowned explorer, the first person to have ever sailed around the globe, then I can't think of a better way to go than to be chased down by natives with spears on the beaches of a tropical island.

I am working on running faster.

I was thinking about Magellan on the first leg of our Brussels Air flight, Monrovia to Abidjan, so I made two short lists for a sermon I was preparing. The first was Places I Don't Want to Die: (1) In a recliner; (2) in line at the DMV (I really don't like the DMV); (3) under a Coke machine (I read recently of a guy who was robbing a Coke machine, pulled it over on himself … and died! I don't want to go that way); (4) hit by a bus (it happens once in a while. There's got to be a better way to go).

My second list was more serious—Places I Wouldn't Mind Dying: (1) Climbing a mountain; (2) saving a life; (3) in the Amazon (never been there but sounds like a good place to be at the end); (4) in the jungle; (5) crossing the Atlantic (be careful what you wish for).

Remember the explosion I mentioned earlier? The BOOM, as the pilot later explained, happened in our right engine. He lost power, the plane pulled hard to the right, and he made the snap decision to abort takeoff.

The pilot hit the brakes hard as the reverse thrusters roared. I, with my seat belt now loosened to the point of being useless, was thrown forward, head first, into the seat back in front of me. One shoe went flying down the aisle. We skidded down the runway. My only thought was, *Man, I hope he can bring it to a stop before we reach the end!*

DO WHAT YOU DO BEST FOR GOD

God gifts each of us with unique passions and abilities. Use them for Him.

I was just in Malawi with Steve Hoesel, a pilot from The Grove who flies for US Airways. He led our team in spending two weeks loving orphans of AIDS. Steve brought stacks of Xerox paper. In every village where they were with kids, he spent his time teaching them how to build and fly paper airplanes. Do what you do best for God.

I just left Nils Wang in Liberia. He owns a large electrical installation company. He spent two weeks wiring building after building for a Christian college that is being rebuilt after the civil war. He must have wired half a dozen buildings in two weeks. Do what you do best for God.

Francis Chan writes about his friend Stan Gerlach. Stan was invited to give a eulogy. After talking about his friend's life, Stan went on to explain in detail what it means to know Jesus Christ as your Savior. Then he ended with these words: "You never know when God is going to take your life. At that moment, there is nothing you can do about it. Are you ready?" He walked back to his seat, sat down next to his wife and sons, slumped to the floor, and died. His family said he left this world doing what he did best for God.[12]

REAL, LIVING EXCITEMENT

Something in the human soul beats for adventure.

After loading the two-thousand-plus pairs of shoes we had collected on Barefoot Sunday into about fifty U-Haul boxes, then into a shipping container we have in The Grove's parking lot, I began to wonder, "How in the world am I going to distribute two thousand pairs of shoes in Liberia?" Then I walked by the desk of our graphic artist, a college student named Joel, and it hit me—dirt bikes!

When Joel and Andre were serving with The Grove in Liberia last summer, a pastor named Thomas Gweh invited them to visit his village in the bush. So Joel and Andre rented dirt bikes for ten dollars and spent the day following Gweh down jungle trails to his home deep in the rain forest. (Side note: Joel crashed—but he healed up fine.) But here was my thought: What if we put together a team of dirt-bike riders who would travel to Liberia next summer and spend every day following Gweh down jungle trails—with U-Haul boxes strapped to the backs of their motorbikes, going village to village giving shoes away to people with bare feet?

I shared the idea of a dirt-bike squad with the people of The Grove, and they loved it. We had our first team meeting for next summer's Africa trip last night, and 123 people showed up. It seemed like half of them wanted to ride the dirt bikes. They'll all go to Africa and serve, but only the best and the finest will get to ride the dirt bikes. I think I should hold tryouts.

God made us to tire of grocery-store lines, traffic jams, Internet downloads, and another senseless episode of *I'm a Celebrity … Get Me Out of Here!* God wants to do so much more in and through you. I invite you today to discover His truly epic adventure for your life.

———

Back to the BOOM on the runway. Right away, we smelled burning rubber but thought it was the brakes and skidding tires. However, a minute later the fire trucks arrived. Our tires were on fire!

Knowing we were loaded with tons of fuel for our flight to Europe, the pilot immediately announced over the intercom, "Evacuate the plane. Evacuate! Evacuate to the left."

My first thought was, "We get to go down the slide! Cool!" (Men are just grown-up boys.) But then the flight attendants opened the doors to deploy the chutes, and the cabin filled with smoke from the burning tires. At the same time, the crew began shouting in urgent tones, "Evacuate! Evacuate! Get out! Get out!"

Well, if you ever start screaming "Get out!" on a burning plane in Africa, know this—you just started a riot. It was pandemonium. People started shoving, women were screaming, babies were crying—it was a free-for-all.

I finally made it to the slide, looked down, and saw a pile of people at the bottom, all getting pummeled by the next person down the chute. I picked a clear spot, held my satchel high, jumped down the chute, and hit the ground running. No way was I going to get kicked in the head by whoever was behind me.

My thought was to get as far away from the plane as possible, but I knew there was a woman from our team in the far rear of the cabin. So I sprinted to the chute at the back of the plane to look for her, all the while thinking, *This is not good. This thing could blow at any second.*

Frantically searching near the rear of the plane, I found her on the ground at the edge of the tarmac, her foot already swollen from hitting the pavement. I helped her up and off the runway, and we headed into the swampy long grass and the dark night, away from the smoking plane.

Now you can stay home, lie on your couch, surf the Internet, keep up the routine … and life is safe that way. Or you can go, give your life away, and let God show you the epic adventure of the life He has waiting for you.

Several hours later, I was in the Brussels Airlines office in the Abidjan airport, trying to get a hotel room for the night, when I noticed a pile of belongings that had obviously been dropped on the tarmac by fleeing passengers: jackets, purses, hats, shoes, and a book titled *Life Wide Open.*

Hey, I thought, *I have that book. Isn't it something that someone all the way over here in Ivory Coast is reading the same book I've been reading? Crazy!* Then it hit me—*Palmer, that's your book, you knucklehead!* It must have flown out of my satchel on my joyride down the inflated slide!

I laughed at myself and picked it up. The cover was mangled, footprints and grime on both sides. As I used my shirt to wipe it clean, I noticed the large endorsement in red on the back cover: "You can bring real, living excitement into your life!" Really?

One chapter in the book opens with six-time Tour de France winner Lance Armstrong's famous words. I love his passion for giving this world all you've got—"I want to die at a hundred years old with an American flag on my back and the star of Texas on my helmet, after screaming down an Alpine descent on a bicycle at 70 miles per hour. I want to cross one last finish line as my … wife and ten children applaud, and then I want to lie down in a field of those famous

French sunflowers and gracefully expire, the perfect contradiction to my once-anticipated poignant early demise."[13]

Give this life all you've got.

Give this world all you've got.

Give God all you've got.

Give your life away.

Ideas for Becoming the Expatriate

Take an Overlander from Cape Town to Cairo.

CHAPTER 8

LEAVE YOUR MARK

Brian quickly approached me as soon as our college worship hour wrapped up. I had shared with the group that our next trip's destination would be Cuba, and I asked them to pray about going.

"Palmer, I'll go on one condition," Brian blurted out. "Promise that I will be thrown in prison, and I will go."

"Why in the world do you want to go to prison in Cuba?" I asked.

"I've been a Christian my entire life," he said, "and I have never been persecuted for my faith. I want to suffer for being a Christian."

"Brian, I'll do all I can to get you thrown in prison!" I promised with a smile.

At twenty, Brian was already weary of the rut. He was tired of feeling like his life did not count for Christ.

You know exactly how Brian felt if you've ever …

felt like you were living on a treadmill,

sat in traffic,

folded piles of laundry,

paid bills—lots of them,

felt trapped in a cubicle,

wanted to quit your job,

waited in line at Safeway,

sat in front of a computer, mind-numbingly delegating spam,

felt stuck in the rut of life

or been in a spiritual rut going nowhere …

and on the inside, your soul screamed, *There must be more!*
There is. I hope you will believe me.

God has so much more He wants to do *in* your life and *through* your life.

I'm convinced an intimate connection exists between going and changing. You open your life to the possibility of transformation when you go someplace else, someplace new, someplace other than where you are right now.

Kyle was in a rut. His life was going nowhere. His soul was numb. Life had turned catatonic. He was twenty-seven years old, working at a fitness club leading routines for the geriatric crowd and soccer moms.

Kyle had been a basketball star in high school, played D-I tennis in college, earned a masters degree—and now life was at a dead end.

He was sitting at our dining room table, wondering how he ended up in this paralyzing grind. My wife, Veronica, and I listened for a while before I said, "Kyle, you need to quit your job, sell everything in your rental home, buy a plane ticket, and move to Africa."

I was really surprised when he said he would think about it.

When he left, Veronica questioned my advice—"Palmer, you can't just tell people to quit their jobs and move to Africa. How do you know that's what's best for his life?"

"I don't," I answered, "but I can tell this—he's dying to be alive."

Less than a month later, I was helping Kyle drag every last piece of furniture out of his rental, including a few items that belonged to his roommates, for a yard sale on his front lawn. He was moving to Africa to serve as the athletic director for a Christian college. We sold about six hundred dollars worth of junk that day, just enough for a one-way ticket to Lilongwe.

Kyle's desires changed. His passions changed. He came alive.

He met a beautiful girl from Cape Town and got married. He's founded one of the largest sports ministries in southern Africa. He's changing lives.

Our conversation over dinner happened more than ten years ago; he's still in Africa today.

IT STARTS WITH GO

The book of Genesis records a great interaction between God and Abram: "The LORD had said to Abram, 'Leave your country, your people and your father's household and GO!'"[1] God gives Abram this simple command—"Go!" He does not say where. He does not promise what it will be like. He just says, "Go!—and I will bless you. Others will be blessed through you. I will use your life in great ways … if you go!"[2]

We often have conditions for God. "When I'm debt free, I will go. When my kids are out of the home, I will go. When I am certain I know where You want me, I will go. When my in-laws have peace about us going, I will go. When there is more stability in that country, I will go."

Famous nineteenth-century missionary-explorer David Livingston once received a telegraph from the London Missionary Society that read, "We would like to send someone to help you in Africa STOP Please inform us if there are good roads to your mission FULL STOP"

Livingston sent this reply: "If the person you are sending needs good roads, please do not send them STOP I need someone who is willing to go where there are no roads FULL STOP"

Practically everything about life today screams, "Don't go!" I hear people say they felt unsafe the last time they visited another country and vow never to leave the United States again. Safety and security seem to be life's driving concerns. But God has called you live differently.

ONE SUNDAY

The front of the auditorium was crowded, lines of people down every aisle. They waited in anxious anticipation to write their names with colored chalk on a black wall. Some held hands, some had quivering hands … because this act was a life-altering commitment. They waited to write their names as a vow to God that they would leave this country to give their lives away for the cause of Christ.

I was floored. I had no idea we would see this kind of response to my challenge: *Give your life away to change this world, and God will change you.*

On one Sunday, two hundred and forty people at The Grove signed their names to say, "I will go and give my life away."

THREE GREAT CHALLENGES FOR THIS GENERATION

Giving your life away to love desperate people was Jesus' idea. He illustrated this expectation by telling of a man who was beaten down, robbed, and left in a ditch to die. His challenge to Christ-followers was to stop—stop and love as He loved.

Today a man lies on the side of the road. His name is Africa. He is a continent beaten down by poverty, disease, and injustice. And if we as Christ-followers have any ambition of honoring God with our lives, then we must respond. This is true religion.

In my opinion, this generation must respond to three great plights in Africa: (1) extreme poverty, (2) disease (particularly malaria and HIV), and (3) injustice (specifically the unjust treatment of women.)

And responding to the pain and problems in Africa begins one person at a time.

ELIMINATING EXTREME POVERTY BEGINS WITH ONE PERSON

The World Bank defines extreme poverty as those who live on less than one dollar a day.[3] For the extreme poor, every day is a fight for survival. Over one billion people live this way, about a fifth of the world's population.

Rhoda Nyreinda is a member of my staff at The Grove, and one Sunday she shared her own hunger story from Malawi:

> Malawi is considered one of the world's poorest countries. Because of this, poverty, hunger, and starvation are everywhere—every night in my home, countless men, women, and children go to sleep hungry.
>
> I grew up surrounded by hunger and hungry people. Here's what it feels like to be hungry: When you're hungry …
> You feel helpless.
> You feel weak.
> You feel shame.
> You feel desperate.

The most desperate are hungry parents—who cannot feed hungry children. Hungry and desperate parents will do almost anything for food.

Recently in my mother's village, a family was starving, literally starving to death. The rain had not come, the harvest was poor, and now they had eaten the last of their maize supply ... even the maize seed for next year's crop.

They had exchanged every possession they owned with the maize sellers for food. Now they had nothing left to give ... so the maize seller suggested they give him their youngest son. The proposal was preposterous, trading their son for two bags of maize.

But, if they did, then the other five children would eat for another month. If they did, they, too, would live to take care of their other children.

When your greatest concern is surviving just one more day, you will do practically anything just to eat.

The parents gave into the burning pangs of hunger—and traded their toddler for two bags of food.

That's what it's like to feel desperate.

That's what it's like to feel helpless.

That's what it's like to be hungry.

———

But here's the hope—extreme poverty can be ended. Global economic experts like Jeffrey Sachs say by the year 2025 we can end extreme poverty. Sachs, a Harvard economist whom some have named "The Smartest Man in the World" has used his "shock economics" to turn fledgling economies around.[4] He is firmly convinced that if affluent nations and people pool their resources—and only 1 percent of our wealth—we can end the plight of the poorest of the poor.

The effort, however, must be massive and concentrated. The reason we have been unable to put out the fires in Africa is that we haven't fought them with enough fire hoses. If your house is burning to the ground, one hose will not put the fire out. But what if you hit the fire with a hundred hoses?

And we don't have to give or do enough to make poor countries or poor people rich; we simply have to do enough to help them get their feet on the first rung of the economic ladder. When countries get their feet on the ladder of development, they generally are able to climb upward. But if a country or person is trapped below the ladder, with the first rung high off the ground, they can't even get started.

Again, it's like being trapped on the roof of a burning building. If a helicopter hovers overhead and drops a rope ladder, you suddenly believe you will be rescued. But what if the helicopter hovers just a couple of feet too high, and you cannot reach the ladder? You won't even be able to get started. But if it comes low enough for you to grab just the first rung, you will most likely climb out of the trap.

And here's where it begins—with you and me. It starts with people committing to give themselves away to changing the plight of hurting people. It starts with one person putting shoes on a man's feet. It starts with churches and clubs and communities adopting one village to give the people there clean water. It starts with companies and businesses putting fertilizers in the hands of farmers. It starts with countries caring about other countries and putting medical facilities in every region.

It starts with one person.

That one person is you.

ERADICATING MALARIA BEGINS WITH ONE PERSON

In many cases, hospitals in Africa are a blight.

When you approach the central hospital in Lilongwe, its perimeter is fogged by smoke from dozens of outdoor cook fires smoldering under the trees. If family members don't come and cook meals for the patients, they will lie in the ward for days without food.

As you walk through the doors, the stench is nauseating. Wards are crowded beyond description. Some patients lie head to toe on a single mattress, some are lain on cardboard under a bed, some are left in the halls. It's not a ward for healing. It's a chamber for dying.

AIDS and malaria in particular have overwhelmed the continent. A child dies every thirty seconds. But here's the kicker—malaria is preventable, malaria is completely treatable, and malaria can be eradicated.

Up until the 1950s, malaria was a problem in Florida, and we eradicated it. Because of United States interest in Panama, we eradicated it there. And if we concentrate our efforts and resources, we can accomplish the same in Africa. You and I can be a part of turning the tide in Africa.

Every time I travel to Africa with teams, we distribute nets, thousands of them. In the scope of things, however, even thousands of nets are only a drop in the bucket when the need is millions. But maybe that's how we can pick the man up off the roadside. One person caring enough to stop, spend ten dollars, and give life to one person.

It starts by someone going to one village and hanging one bed net in one dwelling.

It starts with one person.

It starts with you.

ENDING INJUSTICE STARTS WITH ONE PERSON

An overwhelming mountain of Scripture commands God's people to care for the oppressed. Justice is in the heart of God.

Just weeks ago, a mob of men carried out a judge's order and stoned a young woman to death in Kismayo, Somalia, for the crime of adultery. The stoning was the real crime—a most heinous crime, to be precise. In my opinion, this was the vilest act of injustice I've witnessed in my lifetime—yet the world was silent. CNN was silent. Our president was silent. America was silent. It's not supposed to be this way.

We can't be silent anymore. Ending injustice begins with one person speaking up for those who have no voice, with one person defending the weak.

Here's the bottom line: (1) God hates injustice, and He wants it stopped. (2) Seeking justice on behalf of the oppressed is doable. (3) *You* are part of God's plan for ending injustice in the world.[5]

CHANGE ME

That one Sunday, I had invited several people to say publicly what God had shown them and changed in them when they became expatriates for Him and left this country to take a piece of heaven to hurting people in Africa.

Jarrett said, "The first time I saw children caring for babies, God changed my heart about adoption." Steve the airline pilot followed by saying, "When I came to my first African village, God placed a passion in my heart for hurting people that I didn't even know I had." Jared the college student explained, "While I sat on a bus heading into the Malawian highlands, I sensed God clearly say to me, 'Give your life to ministry.' I have." Darrel said, "The first time I saw peasants drinking water out of a murky swamp and I in turn helped dig a well, I realized one person, just one man like me, can make a world of difference." And Susie shared, "When I spent time in Malawi, 'the warm heart of Africa,' God changed my future forever. I will never live the same."

The global experience will disturb your soul and change your spiritual state. You will have new eyes, you will have a softened heart, you will have an upsized idea of God, you will love people in new ways, you will be bothered by things you never noticed before, you will discover the ability to do things you never believed you could do. Your heart will never be the same.

For two hundred and forty people who wrote their names on a black wall with colored chalk, that one moment, that one act, that one Sunday will forever change the way they live.

Changing this world for good starts on one day—that one day is today.

Changing this world for good starts with one person—that one person is you.

IT'S WORTH THE RISK

When you leave America behind, your identity is solely dependant on the beautiful, dark navy, twenty-five-page booklet with your frightened mug stamped on page two. Next to it is your date and place of birth. And when you are literally thousands of miles away from home, standing in a small concrete building, with the air stale and smoky, in front of an intimidating, belligerent immigration official who accusingly reads the words, "Port Angeles, Washington—where is that?" your mind wildly spins back to the tranquility of your childhood home, which bears absolutely no resemblance to where you now stand. Of course you wonder, *Why did I ever leave?* When he finally hands your passport back, you hold it close to your chest as though it contains life's only hope.

Police are no longer the friendly, chit-chatty guys you joke with at Denny's. You learn quickly to stay clear and as inconspicuous as possible. You don't drink water out of the tap ... anywhere. You seldom venture out at night. There are no such entities as the OSHA, EPA, Better Business Bureau, Bureau of Consumer Protection, or restaurant food inspectors. Forget about refunds. There is no 911, no ambulance, no ER, and no ATM. You are confused by the exchange rate and the need to negotiate a purchase price for everything ... even a Coke.

In spite of all this, God says, "GO!" Yes, go. It's worth the risk. Leave your country, leave your father and mother. Leave your Denali, leave Las Vegas, leave your Starbucks, leave your mother-in-law. Leave the mall and Costco. Because when you burst the bubble that's trapped your soul, you open yourself up to the possibility of God doing something new and wonderful in your spirit. You just might be transformed.

IS IT SAFE?

I've heard the "Is it safe?" question a hundred times from those who test the edges of going global. Recently I was preparing a team to serve in East Africa, and one of the college guys said his mother wanted to come to our next meeting.

As the meeting began, it became clear she had one pressing question for me: "In all these missions trips you have led, has anyone been left behind?"

I guess I really wasn't tracking with her. I thought she meant had I left someone behind in a foreign country much like I sometimes mistakenly left kids behind at Knott's Berry Farm when I was a junior high pastor.

Another team member set me straight—"No, she's asking, has anyone died on your trips?"

Oh, the "Is it safe?" question.

I answered her question something like this: "There are some things I cannot promise when your son goes to Africa. I cannot promise he won't get malaria, yellow fever, or bilharzia. I can't promise there will be no political riots or coup d'états. I cannot promise he won't be held at gunpoint at a police checkpoint or be harassed by soldiers. But I can promise this—I can promise your son's life will be never be the same. I can promise he will be dissatisfied with an ordinary life. I can promise he will see God in a new way. I can promise he will live differently."

She let him go.

DON'T WASTE ANOTHER DAY

Certain images haunt me. The one that frightens me the most is picturing myself old—not debilitated, just sedentary, sitting sleepily in a La-Z-Boy, doing a crossword puzzle, mindlessly watching television. There is nothing that scares me more than to end up with a life wasting away.

But you can waste a life right now; it doesn't just happen when you grow old. Let me tell you how to waste your life. For more than thirty years, Mike of Alexandria, Indiana, has come home from work and painted his baseball with a coat of paint. He began the hobby in 1977 and has painted this single baseball with more than eighteen thousand coats of paint. Mike takes his hobby seriously. He keeps a log and records the time and day and color he paints on the ball. On days when he's feeling ambitions, Mike says he puts two coats of paint on the bulging baseball. Riveting. It's now one hundred and ten inches in circumference and weighs twelve hundred pounds.

You may think this is a joke. It's not. Why in the world would anyone spend a lifetime painting a baseball? I have no idea.

Live with some urgency. This life won't last forever.

In a dream, the apostle Paul saw a man from Macedonia begging him, pleading for him to come share the hope of the Christ with his people. I love what we read next: "We decided to leave for Macedonia at once!"[6] The situation offered no delay.

The ship is sinking. The time to act is now. Waste no time. Stop the wanton pleasure and empty leisure and the fooling around. Get up, get out, and go—God needs you now.

If you've ever prayed about or considered giving your life away globally, then go. Now. Conditions may never be perfect. You can wait a lifetime for the stars to align.

Realize this: God created you with a beautiful, perfect purpose in mind. He intends for you to live a life of significance, a life that impacts people and changes lives, cities, and nations.

Begin each morning asking, "God, in what way do You want me to change this world for You today?" Live that way. Take every opportunity He gives. Walk through every open door … and crash through the ones bolted shut.

When a good friend returned from his uncle's funeral, his first words were, "Wow, that was weird."

"Why?" I asked.

He said, "All they talked about at his funeral were the pepper-tree bushes he raised in his backyard. The pastor talked about the pepper trees. My family talked about the pepper trees. They even had a pepper-tree bush on the podium." His thoughts were the same as mine—is that all his life was about? Raising bushes? That was it?

Value each day. Every day is a gift from God, given to you as an opportunity to serve the world, love people, influence governments, and leave a mark. Live that way, and one day you will hear the words I long to hear: "Well done, my good and faithful servant."

LEAVE YOUR MARK

Not too long ago, Nike ran a full-page ad in magazines across the country. The layout was simple, a full black page with white letters that read:

My name is _____.

I am _____ years old.

My dream is to ...

Leave your mark.

Live to leave a mark for Jesus Christ on this world. Live to leave a mark for Jesus Christ on the lives of everyone around you.

———◆———

I called the groomsmen together in the cramped back hall of the large church, and we waited for the organist to kick into the song signaling the beginning of the wedding I was about to perform for two college seniors from Taylor University. I had the groomsmen huddle around the groom. As we were about to pray, one of the guys (all of whom were Taylor football players) interrupted and said, "Could we recite together, 'What Will Today Bring?' Our football team says these words together before every game."

"Sure," I replied.

So together they recited the following … I would call it a poem, but since they were all football players we will simply call it … "words that go together." I later had one of them write it on a napkin at the reception.

WHAT WILL TODAY BRING?

This is the beginning of a new day.

God has given me this day to use as I will.

I can waste it or use it for good.

What I do today is important, because I am exchanging a day of my life for it.

When tomorrow comes, this day will be gone forever,

Leaving in its place something I traded for it.

I want it to be gain, not loss;

Good, not evil;

Success not failure,

In order that I shall never regret the price I paid for it.

Author Unknown

Ideas for Becoming the Expatriate

Run with the bulls in Pamplona—without getting trampled. You only live once!

PART V

EMBRACE

Love your neighbor as yourself.

It was Christmas Eve. I was lying in a small Malawian clinic with plus-four malaria, sweating and shaking and feeling like I was going to die (actually, malaria rarely kills adults—if you get medication quickly, you only *feel* like it's killing you). Then Mawolo walked into my hospital room with a Scrabble board under his arm.

Mawolo had been a close friend for more than fifteen years. He played on the college basketball team I coached in Liberia. He sat down in a chair next to me and told me he was ready for a game of Scrabble. I turned him down—you can't beat him; he has the entire Scrabble dictionary memorized. Literally. Plus, did I mention I felt like I was going to die?

So he just sat. We talked a bit. Not much. He just sat there to be with me. After several hours, I said, "Mawolo, you can go home now; it's getting late, and it's Christmas Eve."

He said, "No, Palmer, I'm staying with you. I'm not leaving until you leave. We will go home together."

"You can't sit in that hard wooden chair all night, Mawolo. I'll be fine. Go on home," I insisted.

Mawolo refused to leave me alone. He sat in that hard chair all night and waited till morning. He waited until I was well enough on Christmas day to go home; we went home together.

God never meant for you to do life alone.

He designed life to be better when we're together.

CHAPTER 9

KISSES IN HAVANA

Relationships are the fuel of the human heart and the food for spiritual growth. God created all people to be deeply relational. We can easily miss the fact that people around us, people we spend time with, influence our faith. God uses relationships to change us. He never meant for you and me to do our faith alone.

HAVANA

Cubans are naturally gregarious and warm. I've never met a Cuban who, after a hug and a kiss, I didn't feel like I had known for years.

When I took a second basketball team of college students to Cuba, we were invited to a grand, downtown Santiago church to meet hundreds of young people who had gathered to see the basketball players from America. As we walked through the church doors, we were greeted with a barrage of warm hugs and kisses on the cheek from Cuban Christians.

When I finally made my way to the front of the church, I realized the rest of the basketball players were not behind me; they were engulfed by a mob of Cuban schoolgirls greeting them with hugs and kisses. I quickly noticed that I had failed to teach our ball players the fine art of greeting with a kiss in Cuba—the lips and cheek never really meet!

The players (no pun intended) thought they were being good ambassadors by planting a large smack on the cheek of each girl they greeted. The girls were giggling and loving it. They were even circling to the back of the line and starting again!

The first impression we left on the Santiago night grew stronger. One of my players claimed he could speak Spanish, so I sent him up first to give a friendly greeting and represent us well. *Great idea,* I thought.

He began by attempting to say, "Good evening, I am very nervous." Which in Spanish should be, "Buenas noches, estoy muy *nervioso.*" Instead, he took the microphone and confidently exclaimed, "Buenas noches, estoy muy *novísimo!*" Which is, "Good evening, I am the very latest!" The crowd cheered wildly. The teenage girls wholeheartedly agreed. He had a posse of Cuban girls the rest of the week.

RELATIONAL TRANSFORMATION

Groundbreaking thinkers like Lawrence Richards have begun to change the way Christian educators think about learning. Richards believes that people near to us and people who influence us have a far greater impact on our spiritual condition than practically any formal learning experience. Most importantly, relationships can transform the soul.[1]

Former Stanford psychology professor Albert Bandura has also influenced the way educators think about how we learn—and as a result, how we change. Bandura uses the educational principle of social learning theory to explain that people around us have a profound impact on our development.[2] In the case of faith development, relationships deeply influence your spirituality. God created us that way, and it's good.

I don't think I have to argue hard to convince you that much of what we learn does not automatically change the way we live. It just doesn't. We discard far more information than we consciously or unconsciously choose to retain. Environment—the social network of people who surround us—on the other hand, substantially affects our character and the way we live. Do I need to share a clearer example than junior highers? Watch how they dress and talk—just like everyone else on campus. They emulate one another as much as possible. It's the only way to survive. If you don't, you'll be eating lunch alone.

We often travel to faraway places expecting to change people, communities, and countries and miss the fact that possibly the most critical aspect of our going is to connect relationally. We go believing we will change and impact people there through our programs and projects. Maybe. But here's what will also happen—the people there will change you. Open yourself to that possibility. Give yourself to relationships. Allow them to mold your heart. Allow them to transform your soul.

OUT OF AMERICA

I was fortunate enough to spend several years at Biola University studying under Dr. Sherwood Lingenfelter and Dr. Marvin Mayers, two of our country's leading cultural anthropologists. Together they have developed the idea that in order for us to be effective in a global context, we must be willing to become 150-percent Christians.[3]

The idea is this: As Christ left His kingdom in heaven to live the life of a human (the incarnation), at the same time, He took on our humanness. He was fully God (100 percent) and fully human (100 percent). He became a 200-percent person. In a similar manner, we, too, should be willing to sacrifice a bit of our America-ness while also striving to acquire the heart of (for example) an African.

Now, no one expects that you could ever abandon 100 percent of your America-ness, nor can a person from America ever become 100-percent African. But what we can do is forfeit a bit of our cultural baggage, let's say 25 percent, and take on a bit of African culture, maybe 75 percent—to become the 150-percent person.

Peter the Christ-follower finally got it. God told Peter to let go of all his Jewish piety and biases and instead love, in this case, the Italians. Peter resisted; he didn't like the Italians. (This was obviously before calzones, manicotti, spaghetti and meatballs, and deep-dish pizza.) But God insisted. Peter finally got the message, traveled to the home of a Roman commander named Cornelius, and said, "You know, I'm sure that this is highly irregular. Jews just don't do this—visit and relax with people of another race. But God has just shown me that no race is better than any other."[4] Peter's spirituality was transformed. He forfeited his Jewish traditions, embraced the Italians, and became the 150-percent Christian.

If you have aspirations of giving yourself away to this world—and also hope that God will do a transforming work in your life—then allow me to encourage you to consider forfeiting several aspects of your America-ness, or Brazil-ness, or Korea-ness, or whatever your nationality may be, to become the 150-percent Christian.

HEAVEN IS GOING TO BE A LOT LIKE HAVANA

My twin brother and I were crammed in the far back of a Peugeot 505 taxi, making our way back to ACS (the American high school in Monrovia, Liberia) from our home in Yekepa, when the taxi stopped at a checkpoint.

A soldier meandered up, looked inside—and his eyes stopped on us. "You white boys, get outside!"

"My man, I'm not getting out just because I'm white," I retorted. Yes, I was a bit of a punk in high school.

"I say, get outside now!" he demanded. "You are an alien."

Now things got really confusing, because I had never heard the term *alien* used as an immigration status; I only knew of aliens from movies like *Close Encounters of the Third Kind*. But he had a gun, and his eyes were red from the cane juice, so I capitulated and climbed out—all the while complaining and mumbling, "I'm not an alien, I'm not an alien."

But I was.

I grew up in Africa as a minority. And so maybe I've experienced, in just a small way, what it feels like to experience bias, to be singled out, treated differently. It never feels good. But it still happens now, in this country, in your city, and that's not good.

So I say this—of all the places in the world where people gather, the church has to be a place were ethnic diversity is celebrated and promoted. The church is meant to be filled with people from every background. The church (Christians everywhere) reflects God's best when we follow Him with people of other ethnicities, race, nationality, and color. I fully believe the more ethnically diverse a church, the more it reflects God's intention for His people.

Sometimes we give a lot of attention to getting doctrine right—when how we live every day is not right. [5]

I don't know how, but often we miss the fact that God loves diversity. He is a creative God.

I know this because he made Asians and Africans, Samoans and Swedes, Ghanaians and Guatemalans. He made us short and tall, with deep voices and squeaky voices, loud talkers and close talkers.

Heaven is going to be filled with people from every imaginable background. You do the math. About 260 million North Americans profess to be Christians. The count in Asia is about 313 million. The number of Christians in Africa has swelled to more than 360 million. And Latin America boasts a booming 480 million believers! Do you still think heaven is going to be all American? Hmmm.

If heaven is going to be filled with people from every background and every race, then shouldn't the church, shouldn't our living rooms?

When Jesus was here, He settled once and for all the question of *Who is God for?* God is for everyone! He made this point clear when He stopped in the Samaritan town of Sychar and asked a divorced woman for a drink. Her response seems surprising: "You are a Jew and I am a Samaritan woman. How can you ask me for a drink?"[6] She knew the Jews, she knew the culture, and she knew her own sin. She had no business talking to a rabbi.

But Jesus says this: "*Everyone* who drinks the water I give them will never thirst. Indeed, the water I give them will become in them a spring of water welling up to eternal life."[7]

She was different from Him in every way—skin tone, accent, dress, facial features, and sin! She was ethnically, racially, and religiously different, yet He invited her to His home in heaven.

This life-giving water is for Samaritans, it's for single women, it's for the divorced, the lonely, the sinners … this water is for everyone.

Paul picks up on Jesus' thinking and says, "We were all given the one Spirit to drink."[8]

What makes us think this water is *only for me?*

What made us think this water is *only for people like me?*

As I talk about this, one of the things I'm not saying is "become racially blind." No, instead I say, champion diversity, celebrate our differences, promote the blending together of all people of all ethnicities. When God's people come together to worship and work and care and pray, it's a beautiful and God-honoring thing.

I don't believe most Christians are racist. However, the society we live in has created barriers and chasms. Michael Emerson and Christian Smith write about this dilemma and say that the problem Christianity faces in America is that the church is immersed in a *racialized* society.[9] Structurally, we are not *one.* Structurally, we are divided … into neighborhoods and schools and jobs … and churches. As Christians we have to recognize this as a problem and begin to remove these walls and cross these barriers.

Some of you will read this and think, "That's not how I live. I'm not like that." Okay, sure, but maybe all of us, to some degree, have been ambivalent. During an interview, John Ortberg once shared, "When Dallas Willard was once asked, 'Do you believe in total depravity?' He said, 'I believe in sufficient depravity.' That is, when we get to heaven we are sufficiently depraved and nobody will be able to say, 'I merited this on my own.'"[10] In the same way, when it comes to issues of race, we are all depraved, in some way, to some degree, in terms of loving and accepting and including people of every color.

Sometimes Erwin McManus, pastor of the very multicultural Mosaic church in LA, will ask audiences to raise their hands if they work or live in a neighborhood with people of other races. Practically every hand in the room will go up. Then he asks the stinging question, "Will you raise your hand if you have had them over to your house for dinner?"[11]

I think heaven is going to look a lot like Havana.

I say this because on my first visit to Havana, what struck me most was that people of all backgrounds mixed as though they saw no race or color. People of every ethnicity walked together, laughed together, sat in outdoor cafés together, and worshipped together. I had never been anywhere like it.

It was beautiful.

It looked like heaven.

Later, our basketball players were having dinner with the Cuban Olympic team, whom we were playing five days in a row, when one of their players asked one of ours, "Why do you have so much racial conflict in America?"

How do you answer that?

If I were to answer him today, I might simply say, "It's not supposed to be that way. But I will tell you this—heaven is going to be a lot like Havana."

I say heaven will be a lot like Havana because I read that in the final book of the Bible when John describes heaven: "They sang a new song with these words.... 'Your blood has ransomed people for God from every tribe and language and people and nation.'"[12]

I tell the people of The Grove, "If heaven is going to be a lot like Havana, then so must this church."

NOT SO LOUD!

You will never notice how loud Americans are until you leave America. We yell at soccer games, shout at motorists, and scream at graduations. Even the decibel level at which we carry a normal conversation is loud. We don't hesitate to shout directions to the person in the car next to us or talk loudly on the cell phone in a crowded movie theater, and our restaurants are so loud you have to shout across the table to be heard. And try taking your kids shopping at mall stores like Hollister or Zumiez; you can't yell loud enough over the music to be heard.

American homes are loud. With TVs going eighteen hours a day, PlayStation, stereos, dishwashers, AC units, and ringing phones, conversations are tough to have. We live life loud. And so we find it completely normal to greet loudly and speak loudly ... while practically everywhere else in the world, loudness is equated with rudeness.

Even after years in Africa, I recently discovered a new way to be offensive. While coaching college soccer in Malawi, I began the season doing what every good American coach does on the sideline—I yelled at my players. I wasn't yelling offensive or abusive things; I was simply yelling out good instructions, such as, "Hey, Phiri, how 'bout some hustle, you're moving like your grandmother," or "Limbakani, play some defense, your little sister could stop that guy!" You know, just really encouraging things like that.

However, by the second or third game, I began to notice that my bench players would stand farther and farther away from me. And it finally hit me: I was the only one on either sideline who ever shouted instructions at players. Then I realized that no one yells in Malawi, ever. Not even coaches!

PEOPLE MATTER MOST

Westerners are task-oriented. By this I mean that the task at hand matters most, the people involved are secondary. Get 'er done.

Non-Western societies tend to be far more people-oriented. The relationship is much more important than the work.

I grew up in Liberia, where taking time for people is always more important than the task at hand. I once walked into a government office with an American missionary who was still learning the cultural cues.

He walked up to the receptionist and abruptly asked, "Is Mr. Dolo in?"

She kept typing without looking up.

He repeated the question more urgently—"I need to see Mr. Dolo, is he in!?"

She definitely heard him, but kept typing. Now with some irritation in his voice, he almost demanded, "I need to see Mr. Dolo!"

Now she was ready. She looked up slowly, smiled, and asked, "Sir, do you not have 'good morning' in your mouth?"

Ouch. Put people first. Before you can talk business or begin a task you must take the time with the person. Liberians will always begin their time together by asking questions like, "How's the body?" "How's your ma?" "What news?" When all this has been covered, then you can talk business.

When you value tasks more than people, you fail in ministry. Bill was in his early twenties when he first came to the jungle. He was a hard worker and always stayed busy. Soon after he arrived, he was asked to drive a group of pastors back to their villages but was instructed to go only as far as a certain town because the road was too rough after that point. He reached the destination, stopped, and told the pastors they could get out of the truck there. They said, "No, our villages are farther down the road."

Bill heard them clearly, but his instructions were to drop them at this village; his job was done, and they needed to get out of the truck. Now it was a battle of the wills. They refused to get out. His patience was wearing thin.

Did I mention they were in the back of a dump truck? Yes, it's hard to believe, but Bill started the truck, began to drive away ... and pulled the dump lever. Suitcases, briefcases, umbrellas, chickens, bags of rice, and pastors all came spilling out the back of the dump truck.

There's more to it than getting the job done. People matter most.

Bill went back to building houses in Montana.

SLOW DOWN

The West is so concerned with time. The clock and the calendar in our BlackBerrys drive life.

We couch time in economic terms. For example, we say, "I *spent* way too much time listening to her problems." Or, "Stopping to visit the Wilsons when we drive through Omaha will *cost* us too much time." Or, "My time is too *valuable* to waste on his sales pitch." As though time is an asset, a depreciating one at that.

As a result, we cram life full of busyness and leave little time for just being with people. So if you are going to be a global Christian, leave your impatience, leave your agenda, leave your planner, leave your iPhone, leave your CrackBerry, and maybe even leave your watch.

A Kenyan once told my brother Del, "Americans know time," (in others words, they keep track of time well), "but they never have any time. Africans don't know time," (they don't watch the clock), "but we always have plenty of time." Profound.

When we hurry, we rush conversations and minimize people. We nod rapidly so people will finish their sentences. We finish their sentences for them—that's so annoying, isn't it? We literally only listen to a person for seven seconds before our minds begin to wander! Slow down.

Here's the most distinct cultural difference: Events begin in Western society when the clock says they should start. Events in non-Western societies begin when everybody's there. A wedding, for example, doesn't begin at one o'clock because it was scheduled to start at one. The wedding may start at two or three, even though it was scheduled to begin at one. Here's why—the wedding only starts when everyone who's supposed to be there is present, regardless of what the clock says.

If you want to have a lasting impact when you go, focus on relationship. Focus on people. People are life's greatest investment; value them most—because it will be through your relationships that others will be transformed, and you too will be transformed.

BETTER TOGETHER

In his recent book *Outliers*, Malcolm Gladwell observes, "No one—not rock stars, not professional athletes, not software billionaires, and not even geniuses—ever makes it alone."[13]

I'm not good at doing the hard things by myself. And I've realized it's okay to ask others to do the difficult things with you.

I was in the middle of a lecture on spiritual formation when two of our African Bible College students knocked urgently on my classroom door. "Come quickly," they urged. "Someone has drowned in the swamp across the road." I knew the nasty swamp well; I drove past it almost every day. "Can you come save him?"

"How long has he been under?" I asked.

"About thirty minutes."

At that point, I knew I would not be saving anyone, but simply looking for a body. I ran to my car, but before heading over, I stopped by another classroom to find an American teacher named Jason Pink. I said, "Hey, Jason, I know you have a mask and snorkel. Can you grab them and come with me?"

He didn't hesitate. We headed over together.

The student guided us to the edge of the swamp, the scene of the drowning. But strangely, no one was searching the water or even standing on the banks. I expected that a large crowd would have already gathered, as usually happens in Africa when tragedy strikes. We got out of the car to talk to the only person there, a young guy in boxers who was washing his clothes. "Did a boy drown here?" I asked.

"Yeah, I think so," he answered casually.

"What do you mean, you think so?" I questioned.

"You see his clothes there?" he asked. I glanced at the shore and saw a shirt, flip-flops, and shorts.

"He took them off and went in. I was washing my clothes and not paying attention. When I looked up, he was gone," the man explained.

It was one of the strangest conversations I've ever had. I wanted to shout, *If you knew he was underwater, then why in the world are you scrubbing your jeans when you should be searching for a drowned man?! Why aren't you running for help?*

It was all so odd that I asked again, "Is he still in the water?"

"I think so," he answered, seemingly annoyed by all the questions.

"Jason, I guess he's in there. Let's start looking."

I have to be honest—I really did not want to go in that swamp. Forget about the mambas and crocs; I was thinking about the filaria, bilharzia, and blackwater fever I would contract.

The swamp was dank and dark and smelled like stew. But without hesitating, Jason dove in and began swimming around, searching for the young man who had gone under. I waded in along the shore but couldn't even see the bottom. Ten minutes later Jason found the nineteen-year-old boy. He was dead.

As I waded over to Jason and took the boy's arms to help carry him out, I couldn't believe he drowned in three feet of water. As we laid him in the grass, children ran up and told us he had epilepsy.

His death was a result of swimming alone. If just one friend had been near when a seizure turned his body limp, he would have lived. One friend, one person close enough to care, that's all he needed.

We carried him home to his weeping mother.

A year later, I was back in San Diego having dinner with Jason, when he asked, "Palmer, why in the world did you ask me to dive into that slimy swamp? I've wondered ever since what nasty disease I picked up in there."

I joked and said, "Man, you had the only mask and snorkel in Lilongwe; I had to have you." But that was not entirely true. I went on to tell him the truth. "Jason, I simply did not want to search a swamp for a dead man alone." When we do the difficult things in life and for Christ, isn't always better when we do it together?

BETTER TOGETHER

Chalene went to Africa with our team last year. She came home really bothered by the number of children who were alone because their parents had died. She and her husband returned to Africa last month and came home with twin Ghanaian girls. The girls will never again be alone.

Songwriter-musician Jack Johnson writes that, "We're better together." I think he's on to some good theology.

Give up the life alone. We try to do life alone, and it just doesn't work well. God never intended for us to do it by ourselves. It's too hard, and we get lost in our aloneness.

Have you ever had the novel idea, "Hey, I'll go to the movies by myself"? Very bad idea, you realize, once you're sitting in a dark room—alone! Or have you been away on business and needed to get dinner alone? So awkward. Or worse yet, have you tried going to a baseball game alone? Don't do it. You can't cheer alone! It doesn't work. God made life to work better together.

Sometimes we try to make it all about *me*. I think this is why the *i* products are selling so well—the iPod, iMac, iTouch, iPhone. Apple has hit a nerve. Make it just about *me*, for *me,* and it will sell.

We love anything personal. You have the personal computer, personal planner, personal assistant, personal trainer, and you can even order a Personal Pan Pizza. It's just yours. Nobody else gets a bit. "Hey, can I have a slice?" "No, sorry, buddy. It's personal." We even call Jesus our *personal Savior*. That's not a Biblical concept; it's a Western concept.

God is for the community. Look at the Jewish people. God was for all of them. They lived in community, they cared in community, they protected community.

Life is never more complete than when you do it in relationship. A sunset is never so beautiful as when you watch it with someone you love. Fireworks are more brilliant when you watch them with family. A baseball game is always more exciting when you go with a friend. A meal is never so good as when you share it with others. Even a hospital room doesn't seem so bad when someone who cares is sitting next to you—with a Scrabble board.

Ideas for Becoming the Expatriate

Backpack through Europe with your best friend.

CHAPTER 10

SHALOM

This world can be a better place. God wants everyday people like you and me to make this world just a bit more like heaven.

In one small corner of His grand creation, God created a place that was a lot like heaven. He named it Eden. The Garden State was not just beautiful, it was perfect—a piece of heaven on earth. Pain was absent, poverty was unheard of, food was everywhere, and disease was nowhere … and best of all, everybody (well, all two of them) walked close to God.

However, being the humans we are, things went sideways. We tried to deceive God. This one act, this one moment changed everything. This wrongness called *sin* began to spread and multiply and reproduce like a mutating virus.[1]

But here's the good news in all of this—life can still be beautiful.

God is still present, and He's doing good today through people who love Him and want to love others in the same way His Son loved you and me.

We all have this feeling deep in our souls that life can be different, that life can be so much more beautiful than it is. Families are not supposed to be broken. Children are not supposed to be abandoned when their mothers die from AIDS. Fathers are not supposed to lose their jobs. Women are not supposed to be held back because of their gender. And people should never experience prejudice because of their race.

God has a more beautiful way.

John Ortberg, in his deeply insightful way, explains the rich meaning behind the ancient Hebrew word *shalom*.[2] The Old Testament prophets spoke about a coming day when God would change the way things are and make this world beautiful again; to describe this, the Jews used the word *shalom*.[3] The word literally means "to be perfect or complete." When the Jews dream about peace they use the word *shalom*. When King David wrote about peace, he used the word *shalom*. The word can mean *safe*. Or maybe this says it best—*when life is just right*.

A few weeks ago, I was hurrying to a meeting and knew I needed gas but chose not to stop. I didn't make it. The engine cut out on the freeway. Fortunately, I had enough speed to make it down the off-ramp … but now it was uphill to the gas station. When I ran out of momentum, I jumped out and started to push. Cars honked as they slowed to go around me; I'm sure they were just trying to encourage me.

After several minutes of pushing and sweating and not making much progress, a man in a burgundy minivan pulled over, jumped out, and ran over to help me push. "Why isn't anyone helping you?" he asked. I detected an accent.

"Because they're all stinkin' Americans."

He laughed.

We pushed the car up the hill and into the parking lot only to realize that in my hurry getting off the freeway, I had gone right. The gas station was left, on the opposite side of the freeway!

"Get in; I'll drive you over to get some gas," the good stranger offered.

As we headed over I asked, "So where's home?"

"Israel," he answered. "I work for Intel." His name was Ariel (which I later learned means "lion of God").

He asked what I did. I told him I was a pastor. He said he didn't know what that was, so I explained I was like a rabbi without a beard.

"You know, we worship the same God," I offered.

He smiled and shook his head no.

"Really, we do," I objected. "Last Sunday I even taught on a word from the Hebrew Bible (the Old Testament)—*shalom*."

"You did?" he asked, surprised.

"I did. What does the word *shalom* mean to you?" I asked.

"Ah," he answered with passion, "*Shalom* means everything is just right. *Shalom* means life is perfect. *Shalom* means peace is all around us." He paused. "But know this, there will never be *shalom* in my lifetime, or in my children's lifetime, or my grandchildren's lifetime. Never."

"I'm sorry to say this, but I disagree," I answered. "God promises *shalom* to everyone who comes to Him. He promises *shalom* to the Jewish nation. He promises to secure your borders and give you peace. And he promises *shalom* to Gentiles like me who trust Him and turn to Him. Ariel, you can have *shalom*."

He thought for a moment, then said, "Maybe we do worship the same God."

———

Let me tell what this world would be like if we all lived to share God's *shalom* and make the world just a little bit more like heaven:[4]

> *Shalom* means men would stop their cars when they see a guy pushing his car uphill.

> *Shalom* means babies in Africa would sleep under mosquito nets.

> *Shalom* means mothers in Haiti would make cookies for their children with flour instead of mud.

> *Shalom* means husbands would never hit their wives.

> *Shalom* means women in Ethiopia would no longer be sold for sex.

> *Shalom* means women and children would never be chained to trees.

> *Shalom* means girls would never be raped.

And *shalom* means junior highers would never again sit alone at lunch.

God does have a better way, a more beautiful way. And He uses people like you and me to spread *shalom*.

So go and live that way.

Tell fathers to love their sons.

Tell people to love each other regardless of race and ethnicity.

Tell families who are financially desperate that God has a way out.

Tell husbands and wives who feel like giving up on each other that God can put love back together.

He has a better way.
He has a more beautiful way.
A way that begins with you …

taking pieces of heaven to places of hell on earth.

shalom

Ideas for Becoming the Expatriate

Go to Haiti and take shalom.

*Rebuild a home, hold an orphan, teach
school, care for the sick, and love.*

It's your turn.

My name is _____.

I am _____ years old.

My dream is to ...

Leave your mark for Jesus Christ on this world.

NOTES

Intro: One Thousand Percent; Go!

1. Mark 8:34 NASB.

2. Luke 4:18.

3. James Loder, *The Transforming Moment* (Colorado Springs, CO: Helmers & Howard, 1989), 35–39.

4. James Fowler, *Stages of Faith* (New York: HarperOne, 1995), 122–210.

5. Perry Downs, *Teaching for Spiritual Growth* (Grand Rapids, MI: Zondervan, 1994), 73–76.

6. Mark 12:29–31.

7. Bruce Feiler, *Walking the Bible* (New York: Harper Perennial, 2002), 281.

8. John Ortberg, "God's Wisdom is Bigger than My Confusion" (sermon, Menlo Park Presbyterian Church, November 11, 2007).

PART I: EXPATRIATE
Chapter 1: True Religion

1. James 1:27.

2. Matthew 25:35–40 (author paraphrase).

3. Brennan Manning, *The Ragamuffin Gospel* (Sisters, OR: Multnomah, 2000), 51.

4. John 8:7 (NLT).

5. Donal Dorr, *Spirituality and Justice,* (New York: Orbis Books, 1985), 16.

6. Downs, *Teaching for Spiritual Growth,* 97.

7. Micah 6:8 (TNIV).

8. Luke 4:18.

9. Paulo Freire, *Pedagogy of the Oppressed* (New York: Continuum, 1985), 157–158.

10. Proverbs 31:8–9.

11. For more on unresponsiveness, see Bibb Latané and John Darley, *The Unresponsive Bystander* (Upper Saddle River, NJ: Prentice Hall, 1970).

Chapter 2: It's Time to Live Differently

1. Bono, quoted by Scott Morrison (speech, Parliament, London, England, February 14, 2008).

2. Exodus 8:1.

3. Psalm 72:1 (author paraphrase).

4. Psalm 72:14.

5. Luke 9:58.

6. Ephesians 5:14 (NASB).

7. Luke 4:18.

8. Robert Tinker, "Educational Applications of Geographic Information Systems," *Journal of Science Education and Technology* 1.1 (March 1992): 34–48.

PART II: CONFLICT DIAMONDS

Chapter 3: Places of Hell

1. Rob Bell, *Velvet Elvis* (Grand Rapids, MI: Zondervan, 2005), 147–150.

2. Proverbs 24:11–12 (MSG).

3. This account can be found in John 3:1–21.

4. This account can be found in Luke 4:16–30.

5. Ted Ward (lecture, Trinity Evangelical University, Deerfield, IL, 1997).

Chapter 4: Disturbed

1. A. W. Tozer, *The Knowledge of the Holy* (San Francisco: Harper & Row, 1961), 2.

2. Ibid.

3. Isaiah 54:2–3.

4. John 15:5.

5. Sharon Parks, *The Critical Years* (San Francisco: Harper & Row, 1986), 30.

6. Ibid., 74.

7. Ibid., 97.

8. Carol Gilligan, *Moral Development* (San Francisco: Jossey-Bass, 1981), 139, quoted in Parks, 105.

PART III: DO WORK

Chapter 5: Pieces of Heaven

1. James 2:14–18, 20.

2. Psalm 9:1.

3. 1 Samuel 13:14.

Layover: Stuck in Customs

1. Romans 10:13–15

2. Michael Frost and Alan Hirsch, *The Shaping of Things to Come* (Peabody, MA: Hendrickson Publishers, 2003), 18.

3. Shane Hipps, *Flickering Pixels* (Grand Rapids: Zondervan, 2009), 25–26. For more on the idea of "the medium is the message," see Marshall McLuhan's *Understanding Media: The Extensions of Man* (Cambridge, MA: MIT Press, 1994).

4. Frost and Hirsch, *The Shaping of Things to Come,* 18.

5. Brett McCraken, "The Church in a Missional Age," *Biola Magazine,* Spring 2009, 3–6.

6. Luke 14:23–24 (author's paraphrase).

7. Darrell Guder, *The Missional Church* (Grand Rapids, MI: Eerdmans, 1998).

8. Luke 9:58 (MSG).

9. Dan Kimball, *The Emerging Church* (Grand Rapids, MI: Zondervan, 2003), 93.

10. John 1:14.

11. Alan Roxburgh and Fred Romanuk, *The Missional Leader* (San Francisco: Jossey-Bass, 2006), 10.

Chapter 6: Do Love

1. Romans 10:15.

2. This account can be found in Mark 14:6.

3. Psalm 121:3; 91:12; 119:105.

4. Matthew 25:42.

5. Mahatma Gandhi.

6. Will Samson, *Enough* (Colorado Springs, CO: David C. Cook, 2009), 33.

7. Ecclesiastes 7:29 (GNT)

8. Norman Cousins, *Albert Schweitzer's Mission* (New York: W. W. Norton & Company, 1985).

9. Philip Yancey, *Prayer: Does It Make Any Difference?* (Grand Rapids, MI: Zondervan, 2006), 54.

10. Luke 18:20–23 (author's paraphrase).

PART IV: DESIRE
Chapter 7: Overlander

1. Deuteronomy 6:5.

2. Matthew 5:8 (MSG).

3. Ezekiel 36:26 (MSG).

4. Acts 2:37.

5. Downs, *Teaching for Spiritual Growth,* 73–76.

6. Matthew 25:42.

7. Steven Pressfield, *The War of Art* (New York: Grand Central Publishing, 2003), 165.

8. See www.winetowater.org.

9. Ibid., 40.

10. Psalms 39:4–5 (NLT).

11. Ecclesiastes 9:10.

12. Francis Chan, *Crazy Love* (Colorado Springs, CO: David C. Cook, 2008), 44.

13. David Jeremiah, *Life Wide Open* (Franklin, TN: Integrity Publishers, 2003), 20.

Chapter 8: Leave Your Mark

1. Genesis 12:1.

2. Genesis 12:2 (author's parphrase).

3. The World Bank, "Measuring Poverty," http://go.worldbank.org/RQBDCTUXW0.

4. Nina Monk, "Jeffrey Sachs's $200 Billion Dream," *Vanity Fair,* July 2007.

5. International Justice Mission, www.ijm.org.

6. Acts 16:10 (author's paraphrase).

PART V: EMBRACE

Chapter 9: Kisses in Havana

1. Lawrence Richards, *You Can Be Transformed* (Grand Rapids, MI: Zondervan).

2. Albert Bandura, *Social Learning Theory* (Englewood Cliffs, NJ: Prentice Hall, 1976).

3. Sherwood Lingenfelter and Marvin Mayers, *Ministering Cross-Culturally* (Grand Rapids, MI: Baker Books, 1986), 24–25.

4. Acts 10:28 (MSG).

5. Elward Ellis, Robert Franklin, Charles Lyons, John Ortberg, J. I. Packer, Edward Gilbreath, and Mark Galli, "We Can Overcome," *Christianity Today* 44.11 (October 2, 2000).

6. John 4:9.

7. John 4:13–14 (author's paraphrase).

8. 1 Corinthians 12:13.

9. Michael Emerson and Christian Smith, *Divided by Faith* (New York: Oxford Press, 2000), 158.

10. Ortberg, "We Can Overcome."

11. Eric Bryant, *Peppermint-Filled Piñatas* (Grand Rapids, MI: Zondervan, 2007), 122–123.

12. Revelation 5:9 (NLT).

13. Malcolm Gladwell, *Outliers* (New York: Little, Brown and Company, 2008), 115.

Chapter 10: Shalom

1. Jason Locy, "Before the Latch Broke," *Catalyst GroupZine* (Nashville, TN: Thomas Nelson, 2006), 218–219.

2. John Ortberg, *Everybody's Normal Till You Get to Know Them* (Grand Rapids: Zondervan, 2003), 19–20.

3. Cornelius Plantinga, *Not the Way It's Supposed to Be* (Grand Rapids: Eerdmans, 1995), 9–11.

4. The idea for this list comes from John Ortberg's book *Everybody's Normal Till You Get to Know Them,* 20.

5. Eric Jaffe, "The Science Behind Secrets," *Association for Psychological Science Observer* 19.7 (July 2006): 1–2.